School,
BACK TO YOU

A Mom's Guide to Balance and Blessing
in a School Year Transition

A hope*books COLLABORATION

Introduction ©2024 by Brian Dixon

Chapter 1: Educating for Eternal Value: Remember Your Why © 2024 by Jamie Inman

Chapter 2: Building Authentic Confidence: Practical Tools for a Successful School Year and Beyond © 2024 by Keri Lynn Willis, M.Ed.

Chapter 3: Entering the College Drop-Off Zone and Empty Nest: What's a Mom to Do? ©2024 by Anna Dabill

Chapter 4: Joy for the Journey, Wisdom for the Way: A Mother's Reflections on Trust, Growth, and God's Guidance © 2024 by Kayren J. Cathcart

Chapter 5: Loving Your Unique Self: Avoiding the Comparison Trap © 2024 by Énid Meyer Tchir

Chapter 6: A New Chapter Begins: Balancing Joy, Fear, and Faith as Your Child Enters High School © 2024 by Nikki Tigg

Chapter 7: Faithful Foundations: Building Spiritual Resilience for Parents and Children © 2024 by Bonnie Shue McDonald

Chapter 8: Teaching Through Transitions: Balancing Classroom and Home Life © 2024 byTakhia Gaither

Chapter 9: Learning to Let Go When the Road Looks Different: A Mother's Guide to Trusting God with Her Child's Future © 2024 by Amy E. Dyster

Chapter 10: Embracing the Journey: Encouragement + Hope for Homeschooling Moms © 2024 by Chelsea Garofalo

Published by hope*books
2217 Matthews Township Pkwy
Suite D302
Matthews, NC 28105
www.hopebooks.com

hope*books is a division of hope*media

Printed in the United States of America

Thank you for supporting the author's rights.

First paperback edition.

Paperback ISBN: 979-8-89185-200-6
Hardcover ISBN: 979-8-89185-107-8
Ebook ISBN: 979-8-89185-108-5

Library of Congress Number: 2024944512

hope*books
hopebooks.com
Because the world needs your hope-filled
words now more than ever.

Table of Contents

Introduction

A new school year is a time of transition and change, not just for your kids but for you as their mom. Whether you are sending a child to kindergarten for the first time or navigating a new world as an empty nester, it's important to consider how this change affects you and your own identity.

In "Back to School, Back to You," we present a wonderful collection of thought-provoking and inspiring chapters to help you navigate this transition with grace and hope. Each chapter in this collection is a testament to the power of hope and transformation, penned by ten remarkable authors whose words are sure to inspire and uplift.

Here's a brief overview of what you can expect from this collection:

Chapter 1: In Jamie Inman's chapter, "Educating for Eternal Value: Remember Your Why," an eight-year-old boy's curiosity about daily math lessons opens up a profound reflection on the true purpose of education. Jamie challenges the conventional belief that equates success solely with academic achievement and financial security. Through personal stories and biblical references, she argues that education should be a tool for fulfilling God's plan, not just a path to worldly success. Jamie emphasizes the need to align educational goals with eternal values and encourages parents to guide their children in using their educational opportunities to serve God's greater purpose.

Chapter 2: In "Building Authentic Confidence: Practical Tools for a Successful School Year and Beyond," Keri Lynn Willis, M.Ed., shares her personal struggle with articulating accomplishments rooted in a misunderstood sense of humility. Guided by her boss's advice to balance self-recognition with sober judgment grounded in faith, she explores how to foster authentic confidence in children. Keri emphasizes the importance of appreciating each child's uniqueness, instilling a sense of responsibility, and avoiding harmful comparisons. She highlights the value of encouraging a teachable spirit and the impact of respectful communication and proper guidance. Keri urges parents and teachers to help children develop confidence anchored in genuine achievements and self-awareness, creating an environment where confidence can truly flourish.

Chapter 3: In "Entering the College Drop-Off Zone and Empty Nest: What's a Mom to Do?" Anna Dabill shares the emotional journey of sending her first child off to college. She reflects on the years spent preparing her children for independence and offers practical advice for parents facing similar transitions. Anna highlights the importance of teaching essential life skills such as communication, cooking, and financial management to ensure students are ready for college life. She also provides tips for the move-in process and encourages parents to support their children while enjoying their newfound freedom. The chapter concludes with insights on coping with an empty nest, suggesting that parents use this time for personal growth and new opportunities while maintaining strong connections with their children.

Chapter 4: In "Joy for the Journey, Wisdom for the Way: A Mother's Reflections on Trust, Growth, and God's Guidance," Kayren J. Cathcart reflects on the challenges and joys of motherhood through the lens of her children's second-grade science fair project. She shares her initial dread and eventual triumph in tackling the project, highlighting the growth and learning that came with the experience. Kayren emphasizes the importance of trusting God's guidance and finding joy in the journey rather than focusing solely on the outcomes. She encourages mothers to reflect on their progress, rest and reset their priorities, and reignite their passion for the new school year, trusting in God's wisdom and strength to navigate the path of motherhood.

Chapter 5: In "Loving Your Unique Self: Avoiding the Comparison Trap," Énid Meyer Tchir encourages readers, especially students and their moms, to embrace their individuality and God-given uniqueness as they navigate the new school year. Inspired by Psalm 139:13-14 and the story of a girl named Addy who overcomes her fears and thrives in high school, Énid highlights the importance of celebrating one's unique gifts and avoiding comparisons with others. She offers practical suggestions like keeping a gratitude journal, practicing daily affirmations, and setting personal goals to build confidence and self-worth. Énid emphasizes that embracing one's unique path and supporting others can lead to a fulfilling and joyful school experience rooted in faith and self-acceptance.

Chapter 6: In "A New Chapter Begins: Balancing Joy, Fear, and Faith as Your Child Enters High School," Nikki Tigg explores the range of emotions parents experience during this transitional period. She shares her own anxiety and fear about her son's first day of high school, intensified by a fellow mom's comment implying she wouldn't be needed anymore. Nikki reflects on the importance of addressing and expressing these complex emotions rather than suppressing them. She shares her journey of seeking comfort and strength through prayer, supportive friends, and a serendipitous connection with a reassuring teacher. Emphasizing the power of revealing, releasing, and reframing emotions, Nikki encourages parents to embrace this new phase with a mindset grounded in faith and positivity, ultimately finding empowerment and peace in the process.

Chapter 7: In "Faithful Foundations: Building Spiritual Resilience for Parents and Children," Bonnie Shue McDonald shares a powerful story about a frantic search for a lost boy on a beach to underscore the importance of maintaining faith and identity through life's transitions, particularly during the challenging middle school years. She encourages parents to weave prayer, scripture, and community support into their daily routines, fostering a strong relationship with God and modeling these practices for their children. The chapter highlights the need for transparency, communication, and intentional prayer to guide children through their own trials and growth. By developing spiritual habits and seeking mentorship, parents can help their children navigate life's complexities while staying grounded in their faith.

Chapter 8: Takhia Gaither delves into the challenging intersection of motherhood and teaching, especially during and after the pandemic, in "Teaching Through Transitions: Balancing Classroom and Home Life." She candidly shares her struggles with balancing her teaching career and her role as a mother, compounded by the demands of virtual learning and the guilt of missing her children's milestones. Through heartfelt anecdotes and spiritual reflections, Takhia recounts her journey of stepping away from teaching to focus on her family and, later, responding to a calling to return to the classroom. She offers practical advice for managing similar transitions, emphasizing the importance of maintaining positivity, planning ahead, and taking care of oneself amidst the chaos.

Chapter 9: In "Learning to Let Go When the Road Looks Different: A Mother's Guide to Trusting God with Her Child's Future," Amy E. Dyster shares her heartfelt journey through the emotional challenges of raising a child with Asperger's Syndrome and epilepsy. She recounts her fears and struggles as she navigated her son Sam's diagnosis and the anxiety surrounding his transition to middle school. Amy reflects on the need to let go of her expectations and fears, trusting in God's plan for her child. She emphasizes the importance of allowing children to face and overcome their own obstacles while offering unwavering support and prayer. Through her experiences, Amy highlights the significance of staying focused, being a supportive presence, and trusting that God's plan is unfolding for both parent and child.

Chapter 10: In "Embracing the Journey: Encouragement + Hope for Homeschooling Moms," Chelsea Garofalo shares her unexpected path into homeschooling and the deep commitment it requires. Although trained as a teacher, Chelsea never planned to homeschool her children, yet she now embraces it as a labor of love and a lifestyle. She highlights the importance of approaching homeschooling with hope, flexibility, and a clear vision while navigating the challenges with faith and community support. Emphasizing the value of prayer, mentorship, and the freedom to adapt to each child's needs, she encourages homeschooling moms to trust in their journey, celebrate their progress, and find rest in God's promises.

As the publisher, it's my great honor to bring these hope-filled stories to you. These authors have poured their hearts and experiences into their writing, offering wisdom, encouragement, and practical advice to help you navigate your journey with confidence and joy. Whether you're a student, a parent, an educator, or simply someone seeking a dose of inspiration, this book has something special for you.

I invite you to dive into these pages, embrace the insights shared, and allow them to resonate within you. Let's embark on this journey together, celebrating the new season with renewed vigor and a heart full of hope.

Brian Dixon

~ xii ~

Chapter 1

—✳—

Educating for Eternal Value: Remember Your Why

By Jamie Inman

"Why do we have to do math *every day*?"

I glanced down at the pouting face of my eight-year-old son. For all the drama that was dripping from each word, he could have taken the lead in a Shakespeare play.

This was not the first time I'd heard this question whined. It wasn't even the first time this week. We were in the doldrums of our homeschool year. It was February, about the time all homeschool moms wake up early to press their faces to the window glass and watch that big yellow bus roll by while questioning all their life choices. Perhaps my son comes by the drama honestly.

I can't deny that, for a second, I wasn't sure if I knew the answer to his passionate plea. On occasion, I even some-

---

[1] Lewis, C.S. "Christian Behavior." BBC Radio, 1942.

times wondered why math was so all-fired important. My usual answer to this type of query was something mumbled about how we use math in real life all the time, and besides, he'd need it to go to college someday. That answer was never appreciated much, for some reason.

Later, after all the books were stashed away in their space on the shelf, another school day checked off the calendar, I replayed his question in my mind. Why *was* math so important? I mean, really. Obviously, the basics were necessary, but I couldn't recall ever using Trigonometry or Algebra in real life. As my thoughts meandered, they gave rise to more questions. What about school in general? There are kids all around the globe who don't go to school or only receive a minimal education. What about them? Are their lives less meaningful due to lack of "proper" schooling? Is their experience on this earth somehow diminished? There are a lot of folks who would heartily claim education is the key that sets mankind free and ensures a superior quality of life. All of a sudden, I wasn't so sure.

Maybe I was overthinking it. But then again, maybe there was something in this line of thinking. As a follower of Jesus, I have learned over the years that God uses all kinds of people in all kinds of ways. He has a plan and a purpose for everyone. Anyone who draws breath has value to Him. Skin color doesn't matter. Rich or poor, it makes no difference. Tall, short...hairy, or bald, none of that weighs in the balance of a person's worth.

So what about education?

How does that fit into who He made us to be, and does it even matter?

Our society and culture have much to say about the importance of education. Scholastic accomplishments are celebrated, from a Kindergartner's report card lined with "satisfactory" to the elite graduate crossing the stage to receive a doctorate. From the very beginning, we learn that good grades are a measure of our success as a child in school. As we grow older, the pressure often increases. A graduating senior will field a myriad of questions related to the expected furthering of their education.

- *How did you do on your SATs?*
- *Yeah, that GPA ought to land you a decent scholarship, right?*
- *Have you settled on a major yet?*

Parents will encourage and sometimes even push their children towards degrees or lucrative careers. While none of what I've mentioned is wrong or bad in and of itself, I want to challenge our thinking a little bit here for a moment.

I pose this question for you to ponder: *What is my why?*

Why do I want my child to get good grades? *Why* is it important for him to work to keep a high GPA? *Why* am I concerned about her career choice? *Why* is the education of my child so incredibly significant? What is my *why*?

Maybe you've never been challenged to think about the true purpose of education. It's possible that you, like myself, have grown up in a world that doesn't ask this question because they already have their answer. I never asked it, either. For a long time, I regurgitated the ideas I had been fed for decades. It wasn't until I had my own children and started teaching them myself that I began to search for my *why*. What I found changed nothing, yet changed everything.

Allow me to explain.

Challenging Society's Point of View

Do you remember, when you were a kid, planning who you wanted to be when you grew up?

Back then, it seemed the possibilities were endless. And my plans changed almost as often as the tides that swept in and out of the Chesapeake Bay, where I lived as a child.

I remember early on wanting to be a teacher. I adored my elementary teacher. She greeted me every morning with a great big hug, the beads of her eyeglass chain swaying back and forth as she bent down to reach me. School days with her were never boring, and words of encouragement seemed to be her native tongue. She ignited a lifelong love of learning in me. As a young child, she reached hero status in my eyes, and I couldn't imagine a greater life than being just like her someday. It didn't hurt that she raised goats, too. Maybe that's why I now have a herd of seven goats.

Time ticked by, and I was soon caught up in the excitement of a greatly anticipated shuttle launch into space. The Challenger mission was in the news enough for even a kid to take notice. Among the crew was a lady, a teacher no less, and my imagination rocketed. Maybe one day, I, too, could soar into space and visit the stars. It didn't take much effort to envision myself in a puffy, white space suit, peering at the earth through a domed glass helmet.

As I glided into the pre-teen years, I met Jo March in the

worn pages of *Little Women*. I daydreamed of being a tenacious author just like her. I already had no trouble speaking my mind, and the idea of scratching out stories to be published thrilled me to my core. Reading became a passion, fueled by visions of one day being on the other side of the pen.

In high school, I entered my "farm vet" era after reading my first James Herriot book, *All Creatures Great and Small*. Filled with charming stories and words that painted pictures of the dreamy Yorkshire Dales in my mind, I was one pair of Wellington boots away from delivering a lamb in the spring. Eventually, I grew out of this aspiration when I realized I could just read Herriot's books instead. All of the lovely without ever getting my hands dirty or risking life and limb with enormous livestock.

My list of dream jobs was long. How about yours?

The board game *Life* taught me that a career also comes with a dollar amount. As I grew older, I realized the entertaining game wasn't far from reality. If you wanted to make money, you needed a degree. A degree will land you a good job and a good job facilitates a fat bank account. A fat bank account means a happy life. All of this culminates in the dream of enjoying a well-deserved and comfortable retirement. Can I get an "amen"?

We have been trained to believe that money equals security and stability. It means you are a success. With it, you are bestowed a validating stamp of approval from society. You have arrived. This concept was often reinforced by adults in my life along the way as I grew older. I didn't question this line of thinking for quite a while. I'm not going to argue against the reality that this all makes logical sense. We want our children to succeed. Any good parent worth their salt wants a good life for their kids. A better life than we had, usually. We want them to be comfortable. We wish them to have an easier trip around the sun. It's natural.

This is the *why* we have been fed by our culture. Simply stated, we have been told that the doorway to a great life is financial security. The level and quality of our education is the key that unlocks that door. It has become the world's motivation to push and pursue the full extent of educational opportunities.

But what if society got it wrong?

I believe our society's definition of success and a biblical definition of success are two very different things, and therein lies the trouble. When we consider what is really important, we often see that we have become mixed up and confused by looking to the world for answers.

Society says that success is fame and fortune, or at the very least, a life filled with all the good things this world has to offer. Comfort and convenience rank high. Things like a nice house, the right car, trips to popular vacation spots, and all the toys quickly become needs as the ladder is climbed and priorities are set. Pop culture phrases that come to mind are:

YOLO...You only live once.
Grab all the gusto you can.
Eat, drink, and be merry.

A biblical definition of success reads almost the opposite. God's Word tells us to commit our plans to the Lord to find true prosperity (Proverbs 16:3). Scripture clearly says eternity is the end game, not this fleeting life (Matthew 16:26-27). We are admonished to break away from the pattern of this world and find a new one in His will (Romans 12:2).

As I have raised my brood of seven children to the cusp of adulthood, I have seen the alarming adoption of the world's version of success more and more in homes that claim to follow Christ. It has become so easy to accept a mandate from the culture we are immersed in and to feel the need to be successful by their standards. We hardly notice the quiet call from the pages of Scripture to measure our success by a very different standard. The voices of this world are loud, and what they say on this subject sounds very appealing. Defining the terms is imperative if we are going to be able to discern the truth.

Elizabeth Warren, a politician from Massachusetts and 2020 Presidential candidate, affirmed, "A good education is a foundation for a better future."[2] What would be the world's definition of a better future? For some, physical needs may be a legitimate concern, but this quote isn't speaking about humanitarian aid. A better future from the world's perspective is limited to the confines of this physical life.

The truth is, as believers, we do have a better future awaiting us. In John 14:3, Jesus says, "And if I go and prepare a place for you, I will come again and will take you to myself, that where I am you may be also" (ESV). Our eternal future... everyone's eternal future...is of dire importance. A truth we often like to skim over as well in the Bible is touched on in Matthew 8:20. Jesus says, "Foxes have holes, and birds of the air have nests, but the Son of Man has nowhere to lay his

---

[2] Warren, Elizabeth. 2014.

head" (ESV). That passage is one of many where we are gently shown we cannot expect earthly comforts in this lifetime. Our hope, our pursuit, is the promise of the life to come. We cannot embrace a definition of a better future that fails to look past this earthly life and into eternity.

In a speech given on July 16, 2003, former President of South Africa, Nelson Mandela, said these now famous words, "Education is the most powerful weapon which you can use to change the world."[3] It's truly inspirational to think of the younger generation touching the world with new ideas and life-altering innovations. Their success, in a way, is a reflection of our sacrifices for them along the way, and we draw pride from it. Who hasn't at some point marveled at the wondrous possibilities their child's life represents? There is a caution, however, to define the terms. What do we mean by "change the world"? A cure for cancer? Bringing peace to the war-ravaged peoples of the world? Protecting our natural landscapes and resources? None of these things are bad. These are exactly the types of things God *may* use our children to accomplish. But to think this is the culmination of a great education is false. Above all else, we should be helping our children understand that the greatest change this world needs is to be drawn to the Savior. Again, Jesus speaks to us in Mark 8:36, saying, "For what does it profit a man to gain the whole world and forfeit his soul?" When we take up the world's perspective here, we miss the mark.

Many other voices are battling to be heard. I'm just a mom from the sheltered hollers and hills of southern West

---

[3] Mandela, Nelson. "Lighting Your Way to A Better Future." *Nelson Mandela Foundation*, 16 July 2003, Johannesburg. Accessed 1 August 2024. https://www.nelsonmandela.org/content/page/speeches.

Virginia. My voice is small in comparison to the rest of the world, but it's not my words I want you to hear anyway. The Voice we all must be listening to whispers through the pages of Scripture, rustling the pages with the breath of timeless truth. Are you listening?

What Does the Bible Say?

A long time ago, a boy watched over a flock of sheep. It was dirty work. Outside, while the heat of the sun baked the land and the night's cold chilled to the bone, he learned to weather the elements. Wilderness life demanded he practice ingenuity and resourcefulness. Dangers lurked in the shadowy places, testing his courage and commitment to caring for the lambs. Bears stalked and lions prowled, hungry and eager for an easy meal. The young boy had to learn how to defend against their attacks. He grew strong. Scrawny arms thickened as sinewy muscles bulked from carrying injured sheep. Skin darkened in the Mediterranean sun. In moments of peace, when the work of the day was finished and the sheep safe, the boy picked up his harp, pacifying the herd with songs as he increased his skills with the stringed instrument.

Have you guessed the identity of the boy?

David, the ancient shepherd king of the Old Testament, received an education that wasn't much to our modern way of thinking. His scholastic achievements were meager, to be sure.

- He majored in Shepherding.
- He minored in Music, with an emphasis on the harp.

- He passed "Sheep Defense 101" with flying colors.
- His workshops coached on leading lambs to green pastures and finding still waters.
- All with instant practical applications.

It was not the education of a royal. He wasn't schooled in etiquette and language. David wasn't tutored in matters of state or political maneuvering. He didn't receive training as a general or in tactical warfare.

But God used the education David received on the grassy hillsides of the country to unite a kingdom and secure the borders of His people. The lessons learned as he faithfully tended sheep made him a great king. When Samuel the prophet broke the news to Saul that his line would end and David would take his place, he said in 1 Samuel 13:14, "...The LORD has sought out a *man after his own heart*, and the LORD has commanded him to be prince over his people...." (ESV, italics mine). God's man, being used in God's plan.

David's education was a *tool* God used to play out His grand design for David's life and the course of Israel as well. The weaving of the story of David even includes a direct line right down to the Messiah Himself, Jesus. All that from a little shepherd boy.

There are countless other examples in Scripture of God using the opportunities He gave individuals to further His plan for them. Joseph had a tough road to walk, but he learned valuable lessons along the way that set him in a position to change the course of his family's future. Peter's time learning the trade of fishing served him well as the Master, passing by one day, reached out His hand and invited Peter to join him to fish for men. The apostle Paul had a stellar education for his time. He was highly respected and was climbing the ladder of success among his religious peers, only to be stonewalled by a blinding light. The Voice of the one he thought was his enemy but turned out to be the Savior of his soul. The call to change sides was a shock to everyone, most of all Saul, as he was called then. Yet his credentials are what made his testimony and ministry so powerful. (See Philippians 3). God used the education self-righteous "Saul" received to empower the apostle "Paul" to spread the gospel.

There was nothing extraordinary about these fellas. They were just people. Some poor, some perhaps wealthy. They had varying degrees of what the world would call success. Yet, they speak from the past, something we need to know in this age. God's version of success looks very different from the world's. Despite their spectacular ordinariness, God equipped them and called them into His service. He had something for them to do and made sure they had the training they needed to accomplish the task. It may not have made any earthly sense to train a king in a pasture of sheep, but God knew the end of the story before David was even written on the first page. All these men had jobs that transcended the boundaries of their earthbound lives. The kind of work that pays out in perpetuity. Eternal paychecks.

There is a hunger we all feel for something more. Something beyond this life. It's placed deep in our hearts from the very beginning. We have it. Our children have it. It's a longing for eternity, even while we ride in the car, work on a Monday morning, or eat dinner with friends. The deepest part of who we are is drawn to seek purpose for our lives. Solomon, David's boy, penned these words in Ecclesiastes

3:11, "He has made everything beautiful in its time. Also, *he has put eternity into man's heart*, yet so that he cannot find out what God has done from the beginning to the end" (ESV, italics mine). A longing, a purpose, known by God. We place our future in His capable hands and watch His plan unfold page by page. And we pass these truths to the next generation (Proverbs 22:6).

The education our children receive is a stewardship opportunity. In 1 Corinthians 4:2, Paul tells us what our responsibility is when he states, "Moreover, it is required of stewards that they be found faithful" (ESV). Faithful. Faithful to take the opportunity, the gift, of our education and our children's education and use it for the Lord. It is an **investment** God is making in us. The purpose we search for can be found in using the gifts we are given in service to the Lord. We are His. Loved and cherished, gifted and enabled to live the life He has called us to. Our kids need to know this truth.

When all is said and done, when we stand before the Lord God and account for our stewardship of all the things He gave us, what will we say? Will we be able to give testimony of a life given in service? Or, will the truth be that we spent all of our opportunities on our own selfish desires? Weighed in the balance, does the temporary outweigh the eternal?

These questions are simple but hard to answer honestly. Often, the truth is ugly. My own mirror frequently reflects an image I don't want to see. A life of service is not a popular choice in a world that worships the idol of self.

What the world doesn't understand is that there is freedom in sacrifice.

There is blessing in service.

There is peace in purpose when it's ordered by the Lord.

Handing over our plans for life and allowing God to use education to further His plan is the only way to find true success.

A New Point of View

It's time to change how we see school.

The education of our children is not the foundation on which we build a future or a world-changing weapon. The education of our children is a tool. It's made to serve a purpose, like many other tools we may use.

I love to steal my husband's tools. It's true. I am a thief. On occasion, I've been known to sneak down to my husband's side of the basement and browse my options when I feel the urge to hang a new picture or fix something that's broken. I have an obsession with those screwdrivers that have all the interchangeable heads. I love how each tip stores neatly in the handle. Genius! I can't help it that after I use it, the tool somehow ends up in my kitchen drawer. Can you blame me? My better half eventually caved and bought me my very own power drill set, hoping to minimize my klepto habits, but I still like to pilfer the occasional hammer or screwdriver. I consider it a compliment to his good taste in gadgets. His tools are so cool.

I never really thought about tools much growing up. They were always around because, for a while, my dad was a general contractor. It wasn't unusual to hear the scream of a circular saw drifting from the shop behind our home in the afternoons after school. I remember helping him stain trim, long strips of beveled wood strung between two sawhorses in the backyard. That was when I learned there are different paintbrushes for different types of painting. Tools were a common fixture in my world growing up.

Then, after graduating high school, I had the opportunity to travel to South America for a three-week mission trip. After arriving in the capital city, we took a tiny Cessna airplane into the heart of the jungle. That was followed by a three-day canoe trip deeper still into the endless green sea of trees. It was remote. The goal was to help finish an airstrip so that future visitors could skip the lengthy river journey. I quickly discovered the tools used in the jungle are not the same tools used in suburban America. I recall machetes being a tool of choice. I'm sure there were other options, but there were no big power tools or other implements we would consider necessary for that type of work. Without a source of power, they would have been nothing more than expensive curiosities. The people whose land we were visiting were skilled in wielding their implements and accomplishing the work at hand with the tools available to them. They were good stewards of what they had been given.

Why do I tell you these stories? It's simple. There are different tools for different jobs, and a tool is only there to help accomplish a purpose. As shiny and enticing as one might be in and of itself, its only true value is in whether it accomplishes its purpose or not. And not everyone owns the same tools. The natives of the South American jungle had probably never seen a hydraulic wood splitter or a lithium-ion circular saw, and yet they still found a way to carve out a town of houses and a runway for planes with the tools available to them.

Education is a tool.

It's a tool that God uses in the lives of His children to further His kingdom.

As a follower of Jesus, we must break free of the false narrative the world proclaims. The aim of education is not to better our kids' future here on earth with high-paying careers, the latest tech, and all the comforts this life may afford. Its purpose is not to provide peace of mind in financial security. It is not the end-all, be-all solution to a world filled with social ailments.

Believers are not promised financial security. We are not promised all the fixtures and trimmings of a comfortable life. If we look at examples from Scripture, we see something quite different. Our investment is in eternity because this present life comes with a steep price tag.

> "Do not lay up for yourselves treasures on earth, where moth and rust destroy and where thieves break in and steal, but lay up for yourselves treasures in heaven, where neither moth nor rust destroys and where thieves do not break in and steal. For where your treasure is, there your heart will be also."
> Matthew 6:19-21, ESV

These verses talk about keeping eternal values in view. If our hope of treasure rests in this life alone, our aim is off.

The truth is, some of us have more to steward than others. American society has access to so much when it comes to how we educate our children and to what extent. We have been given many opportunities to be stewards of our education. The children living in a hut along the banks of the Amazon have a much different stewardship challenge. Not less, just different. In both cases, the Lord is going to require faithfulness.

Remember a few pages ago when I said nothing changed, but everything changed? Here's how.

Aligning your point of view regarding education with God's eternal perspective doesn't change anything tangible. Your child will still go to school. Your child will still face the question of colleges, trade school, or no higher education at all. Your child will still need to make decisions for the future that involve job interviews, paychecks, raises, and career changes.

So what **does** change? Your entire perspective! And hopefully, you can then direct your child's perspective as well. As they question the reason for math or get weary of English grammar, when they don't know what college or degree to choose, keep reminding them of God's greater purpose. Whisper words of encouragement that the education they're gifted with is a wonderful opportunity He will use in their life as they follow Him. They must use it wisely. They must use it well. They must not squander their abilities or waste their talents.

Ask God how He wants them to use the gifts He has given. Maybe He wants your child to be a neurosurgeon. Maybe He wants your child to be a mechanic. Maybe your child will have no official career at all, like that of a homemaker. The important factor is that your child is serving the Lord with their life, stewarding the educational tools He's brought their way.

Conclusion

As you enter this new school year, take a moment to consider your "why." In the whirlwind of popular opinion and society's pressures, there is a still, small voice speaking words of truth. This life is more than what we see and stretches farther than the confines of time itself. Education? It matters, but not in the way we've all been led to believe by our culture. It's time to start a fresh, new year of school with a fresh, new perspective: one that will last for all eternity.

Back to School Liturgy

God in heaven,

Let us treasure You above all else.

Your Word is our light for the path and the lamp for our feet.

As we set our hearts on eternity while firmly planted in this world, may we see each earthly opportunity in its eternal perspective.

With each new school year, help us to lay our courses down before You.

Teach us how to be good stewards of the gifts, talents, and tools You bless us with so that when our fleeting time is over, we might hear Your voice say, "Well done."

Amen

Questions to ponder:

1. Are you being faithful to steward your education well? What are the opportunities God has given you?

2. Are you passing that mindset on to your children? Not all opportunities are equal. God gives different portions to different people. The amount you're given to steward doesn't really matter. What you *do* with it does matter.

3. Read Matthew 6:19-21. What are your treasures? Do you need to reconsider what your treasures should be?

Chapter 2

✳

Building Authentic Confidence: Practical Tools for a Successful School Year and Beyond

By Keri Lynn Willis, M.Ed.

Stumped, I sat at my boss's desk. I was supposed to submit a report detailing my accomplishments for the year. I had made good contributions to the organization but could not articulate what and how. My boss knew I had achieved my goals, but my job, largely independent, required me to lay out the details. Confused, my boss asked why I had such an issue with this assignment.

"Do not think more highly of yourself than you ought to think," was the only logical answer I could give. She studied me and said, "Keri, that isn't the whole verse," then finished it for me. "Think with sober judgment according to the faith He has given you."

She encouraged me that it was good to be confident, acknowledge the work I had done, and find satisfaction in knowing I had done it well.

I grew up believing that verse meant I had to think poorly of myself, and anything else was pride- the bad kind of pride. I believed I couldn't take credit for my work. There was a bar set so high I would never be able to reach it, and if I did, I certainly could not look back at my work and say it was good.

Not only *can* we look at our work and feel good about it, but Scripture tells us, "Pay careful attention to your own work, for then you will get the satisfaction of a job well done..." Galatians 6:4a (NLT).

Teaching and achieving authentic confidence are lifelong challenges. Throughout our lives, we need a balance of affirmation and correction to ensure that we effectively use the gifts we have been given and do the work we are called to do.

Most assume kids will outgrow wavering confidence, but it can last a lifetime. What we say, how we act, and how we evaluate their performance can impact our children forever. Small successes can build confidence. Parents and teachers can help individuals see their value and success in everyday events and have the joy and responsibility to train and build up children.

How can we ensure our children are confident enough to be successful but not so confident they become a bully or have false confidence, setting them up for failure? First, we must understand what authentic confidence is, taking care to build steps into our everyday activities, conversations, and attitudes, constructing confidence that will accompany them into adulthood.

Throughout this chapter, I will share lessons I've learned as a child, a parent, a teacher, and a school administrator about the need to grow authentic confidence in yourself, your children, and your students. In full disclosure, I have struggled with confidence most of my life, but by God's grace, I've accepted and embraced myself for who God made me to be and the work He has laid out for me. One of my greatest joys is instilling that gift of confidence in students who struggle to function and fit in.

1. Understand Authentic Confidence

By definition, authentic means real, true, accurate, and genuine. Confidence is the feeling of trust that something or someone is reliable. Authentic confidence means understanding the truth about our unique skills, abilities, personalities, and accomplishments. We also understand our failures in a way that helps us know how to grow, build on, develop those skills, and learn from our failures. It is 'thinking with sober judgment' about the gifts and faith given to us by the Master Teacher. Sober means nothing is impeding our ability to see ourselves as we really are: children of God, made in His image.

Building authentic confidence requires helping children identify their uniqueness, strengths, and weaknesses and building on them, gently correcting and looking for growth along the way. We must do everything possible to give them a safe community, allowing them to learn from their mistakes. A false sense of confidence comes from misguided rewards and fabricated praise.

Look for advice and wisdom in the right places. With a barrage of advice available, you may ask yourself, "What are we supposed to believe?" There may be some good information out there on Instagram and TikTok, but that is not where true wisdom abounds. It is where self-aggrandizing and a plethora of false confidence reigns. A million followers on social media does not make one an expert. If you hear something you think is a good idea or even a bad idea, test it through the lens of Scripture.

Is it true, honorable, right, pure, and just (Philippians 4:8)? Will it build up a false confidence in your child (Romans 12:3)? Will it hurt them spiritually, emotionally, or physically (I Thessalonians 2:11-12)? Is there a potential for causing bitterness (Ephesians 6:4)?

2. Carefully Build Authentic Confidence

There is no magic formula for building authentic confidence in our children. Doing so takes prayerful, consistent, loving, patient, and kind discipleship. It requires a moment-by-moment, day-by-day investment in the most precious gift ever given to us, our children.

Pray with and for your child. Knowing and trusting God builds courage and confidence. Teaching them to pray for others makes a difference in how they handle the ups and downs of relationships.

Treat children with respect. Recently, one of my former students pointed out that she thrived in my classroom because I listened to them and treated the class with respect. Adults say some horrendous things to their children. "I hate you." "You're stupid." "Nobody would want to marry you." Sticks and stones may not break bones, but they can destroy, leaving permanent wounds and scars. We are told, "Do not let any unwholesome talk come out of your mouths, but only what is helpful for building others up according to their needs, that it may benefit those who listen." Ephesians 4:29 (NIV). We are also told in Proverbs 15:1 and Colossians 3:21 that harsh words will crush the spirit. We must use our words to mold and build those spirits, not break them.

Embrace unique qualities. At the beginning of every school year, I tried to ensure my students understood that I valued them as unique individuals and that there was no 'normal' to achieve while sitting in my classroom. I expected them to work hard, do their best, follow reasonable and clearly outlined classroom protocol, and honor God and each other with how they spoke to and treated those around them.

Resist the urge to compare. One of the greatest detriments to building confidence is the comparison game. Even as adults, we struggle with seeing someone's great life on social media. We look at others' success, new car, new home, perfect marriage, perfect children, and think, "Why can't I be more like them?" I've been there and still wrestle with it at times. The change in me came when I grasped that my confidence is in who I am in Christ, how He calls me His own, and has uniquely gifted me for the work to which He calls me.

As a classroom teacher, I had a front-row seat as the comparison game played out daily. To combat this malady, I had this verse posted right by my front door:

"Pay careful attention to your own work, for then you will get the satisfaction of a job well done, and you won't need to compare yourself to anyone else. For we are each responsible for our own conduct" Galatians 6:4-5 (NLT).

While extremely challenging, it is so important for parents to view each child individually. "Jani is our 'C' student," her parents stated plainly as they sat across from me at her parent-teacher conference. Shocked, I tipped my head in question to the parents of one of my brightest and most enthusiastic fifth graders. Jani was the youngest child of parents who had diligently homeschooled their older children. However, they were waning in their enthusiasm with their last and maybe most challenging child. She perplexed them because her intelligence did not fit her parents' idea of an ideal student. They did not 'get' her learning style or natural gifting. She was a right-brain thinker – very creative, dramatic, and artsy, while her older siblings and parents were all studious academics. Jani was 100% as capable and intelligent as her older siblings. Her abilities, strengths, and gifts were manifested in a completely distinctive way and caught her parents by surprise. They were trying to teach her in the same 'color in the lines' way in which her siblings thrived but were killing Jani's confidence and limiting her success.

As parents and teachers, we need to model contentment in who our children are created to be and have a desire to see them grow and succeed. We cannot expect them to be someone they are not created to be. It is likely that, as adults, we still remember some of the damaging comparisons we experienced as children.

As an elementary student, I was always the shortest and youngest student in my grade. Inevitably, when it came to the time of year when we were learning descriptive adjectives, I was called to the front of the room along with Jerry, the tallest kid in the class. We would stand there while the teacher systematically compared us.

With every comparison, I felt smaller and smaller because I heard, "Keri is short. Therefore, she is less than Jerry. Jerry is smarter; Jerry can do more than Keri; Jerry has better parents because they must be tall, too." While none of those last comments were actually made, that is what my little third-grade mind told me, and I assumed that is what the other students heard as well. Children are interpreters, and often they get their interpretations wrong. What the teachers can mean as a simple lesson builds one student up while tearing another down. If a comparison is necessary, let it be a big cookie vs. a small one or a Redwood vs. a Bonsai.

"But the LORD said to Samuel, "Do not look on his appearance or on the height of his stature, because I have rejected him. For the LORD sees not as man sees: man looks on the outward appearance, but the LORD looks on the heart." I Samuel 16:7 (ESV).

Comparing children or ourselves is a dangerous road to travel. It is destructive and goes against God's plan for our lives, joy, and well-being. We need to invest ourselves in building up our children's hearts, faith, and confidence in who God created them to be.

Teach the difference between being 'sober' in our judgment and being proud. Throughout scripture, we see pride as a detriment, not a benefit. We are told not to think too highly of ourselves and to consider others before ourselves. But we want our children to feel a great deal of accomplishment in their work. We want them to have confidence that will aid in their success. So how do we strike the balance necessary to make them kind, humble, and gentle while attaining that confidence? The idea of 'sober judgment' implies that we need to look at ourselves and others through the eyes of the God who created them to be uniquely gifted individuals.

Here are some concrete ways to build authentic confidence in your child:

- Appreciate your child's uniqueness.
- Avoid rewarding children for something they didn't earn.
- Be careful not to teach them to think they are better than others.
- Don't tear them down, discourage them from dreaming, or make them feel less than who God created them to be.
- Don't tear down any other child to make your child look or feel better about themselves.

For example, do not say:

- "I am so glad you got all A's on your report card. I bet Sally didn't."
- "I see you got all B's on your report card. Why didn't you get all A's?"
- "I am so glad you got first place in the spelling bee; you are clearly smarter than any of the other students."
- "Why didn't you make the team? Sally did, and she isn't even as good as you?"

Do say:

- "I am so glad you got all A's on your report card. Your hard work really paid off."
- "I am so glad you won first (or second or third) place, I love to see your hard work rewarded. I hope the other students enjoyed being part of the program and feel good about how hard they worked, too."
- "I am sorry you didn't make the team. Maybe I could help you practice if you want to try again next year."

Help them learn to deal with disappointment without discouragement. Teach them to forgive if they think their disappointment is at the hands of another but seek justice if necessary. Give them tools to improve if that's what they need. It is great to acknowledge hard work and accomplishments, even celebrate them, but for the child who does not easily get good grades, win competitions, or make the team, we need to find ways to acknowledge their milestones and accomplishments just as much as the child who always wins the awards.

My adult daughter loves to fish. When we go out on the river, she catches more than anyone else. She also casts her line more than anyone else. She does it over and over again. She didn't catch much when she first started fishing. If she had become discouraged and given up because she wasn't successful at the beginning of her fishing experience, she wouldn't have become the skilled angler she is today.

We need to encourage our children to keep working hard, try new things, and not take failure as the 'final grade' but as a stop along the way that gives course correction.

Help them build a solid academic foundation. Reading, foundational to academic success, does not come easily to every child, but with few exceptions, it is something every child must learn to do. To become confident readers, students must read and read a lot.

Reading silly books can help your child learn to enjoy reading, which will, in turn, build their comprehension, confidence, and overall school success. If they find a book or series they love, as long as it is appropriate, encourage them to devour it. One parent was discouraged because her son only wanted to read A *Series of Unfortunate Event*[4]s for his required reading. I asked, "But he is reading, right? And is he reading without you prompting him to? And is he completing his work?" "Yes," was the answer to all three. She could hardly get him to put the book down. I suggested that even though there was not a lot of substance to what he was reading, he was building reading confidence, reading fluidity, and most importantly, reading enjoyment. She ended up negotiating with him so he could read his silly book before he did the rest of his homework and then reward himself with more of it when he finished. I think he eventually became an engineer.

Help them find ways they will use what they are learning in real-life situations. Read road signs. Look for interesting plaques in parks. Take them shopping and let them add up how much money you're spending along the way or how much tax will be. Compare it to how much you have budgeted. Plan cooking projects that grow in complexity as your child matures.

In my 4th - 6th grade classrooms, I had a 'token economy.' Everyone started the day with four class bucks. They

---

[4] Handler, Daniel. *A Series of Unfortunate Events: The Bad Beginning*. HarperCollins, 1999.

could spend bucks on talking, coming in late because they chose to play instead of using the restroom, talking when they should be listening, etc. At the end of the week, they could deposit their bucks into the 'bank,' and once a month, we had a store where they could purchase items with their earned 'funds.' Occasionally, a student had to pay another student with their class bucks if they had acted irresponsibly towards that student. Students knew the expectations and enjoyed the challenge of managing their behavior and finances. This taught responsibility and gave value to showing up and doing the right thing. Building confidence and responsibility is easier if you make your expectations clear, reasonable, and consistent.

Encourage them to take responsibility for their work, actions, and attitudes. Redirect blaming. If there is really a problem with the teacher, curriculum, or other malfunction, address it. However, it will be most beneficial for your child to be responsible even when they don't like or appreciate a particular subject or teacher.

When appropriate, **allow your child to make decisions,** and allow them to accept the consequences, good and bad. It may be as simple as picking out clothes for the day or what kind of sandwich to put in their lunches, but small decisions will build confidence for making more important and potentially life-altering decisions. It also gives the strong-willed child freedom within boundaries.

One of my best teaching moments as a parent was after Halloween. In the third year of carefully curating how much candy and when they could eat it, a protest broke out. "You never let us eat our candy," was the battle cry. After a few rounds of the very dramatic scene, I said, "Okay, knock your-selves out; eat all you want." And they did! The next morning, I heard, "Oh, mom, why did you let us do that? My stomach hurts, my head aches." I don't like kids to make decisions that will hurt them, but in this case, it helped them learn a valuable lesson. There were reasons for the 'rules,' and it was for their benefit. Having what we 'want' isn't necessarily what we 'need' and is frequently not what's best.

Help your children have a teachable spirit. Part of en-couraging a teachable spirit is nurturing curiosity. Encour-age them to explore new activities that broaden their in-terests and habits. Find opportunities to build on naturally developing curiosities. A child who loves to build with Legos may become an architect. One who loves animals may be a vet or vet tech. See and acknowledge both the little suc-cesses and the major milestones, and help them find the ac-tivities, subjects, and projects in which they thrive. Reward success and help them learn from failure. Answer the frus-trating question, "WHY?"

Always keep learning and let them see you learn. Be transparent with your children. If you don't know the answer to a question, tell them, "I don't know; how about if we work on finding the answer together?" "I am not sure about that, can I think about it and get back to you?" Let them see you take classes, read, do research, make mistakes, learn from them, and celebrate successes.

Teach them problem-solving skills and allow them to 'reach.' Watching my seven-month-old granddaughter play was so much fun. I sat on the floor and took out one toy at a time for her and put others away as she was done with them.

I handed everything to her until I saw her reach for something beyond her grasp. My first inclination was to pick it up and hand it to her. But something stopped me. I realized that by handing her everything, I removed from her the opportunity to discover and explore on her own. I knew I needed to let her reach and stretch her body and mind in solving a very simple problem. This way, as she develops, she will continue to solve her own challenges rather than wait for someone else to give her what she wants or needs.

Help your child know when to ask for help and when they need to figure things out independently. Allow them to make decisions, increasing in complexity as they grow and mature.

Allow them to play and discover. Somewhere in the long history of education and child development, a misnomer was perpetuated: learning is hard and not fun. But, to the contrary, learning can and should be fun. Sometimes memorizing a list of dates, events, or people is necessary, but if you add a song, a cooking project, or a craft, it becomes less painful, and the information sticks better because you have connected it to real life and given it an anchor.

Almost 25 years later, one of my students recalled sipping a "Mississippi Mud DeSoto" (root beer with chocolate ice cream) while learning about DeSoto discovering the Mississippi River. Your kitchen is the perfect place to teach fractions through simple or complex cooking projects. It is also an ideal science lab to teach solids, liquids, gas, chemistry, and, of course, safety! Help them understand it is okay to make a mess and make mistakes along the way, and when the 'project' is over, look at it and declare, "It is very good!" If it isn't very good, encourage them that it will be better next time.

Learn with your child that something that can be very fun will often also be hard work. And that is okay. God created us to work. In a perfect world, work was always pleasant, but in a fallen world, it isn't always so. We started backpacking with our children when they were seven and nine years old. I remember the grumbling along the way (some of it may have been my own) about the hard work we had to do and the high mountains we had to climb. We went to places you can only get to by hiking and saw some of the most majestic scenery and animals God ever created. None of this would have been possible if we hadn't worked hard to get into physical shape, planned, and packed efficiently with the supplies needed to survive a week in the wilderness. Even though it was hard work and there was grumbling along the way, inevitably, one of us would proclaim, "This is the best vacation we have ever taken."

Mold the strong will. Strong-willed children can challenge the best of us, but they are a special gift entrusted to us by God and, if given proper guidance, will flourish. We walk a tightrope. We want to build them up, but we don't want to make them overconfident or bullies. We need to correct them but not discourage them. We want to give them what we didn't have growing up but not spoil them. We need to teach them a good work ethic, but we must have reasonable expectations for each developmental age. **We need to mold their wills, not break them.**

Allow correction by other respected adults, but never abuse. And help them understand the difference. In response to abuse in homes, schools, and churches, there has been a backlash by parents trying to protect their children. I am a fierce protector of children. But when children outright state or have an attitude of, "I don't have to do what you tell me," it makes being their teacher next to impossible. An authentically confident child will feel empowered to say "no" to potential abuse without feeling the need to defy appropriate authority. We don't want our children to blindly obey every adult because this can be very dangerous. **We need to teach our children respect with good boundaries.**

Guide them in dealing with injustice. Encourage children to share when they feel there has been an injustice and help them know how to address it correctly. Help them to see the situation from different perspectives. Ask questions and listen for the answer, spoken and unspoken. Pray for wisdom to know if it is something they can handle with some coaching or if you need to step in and offer assistance or intervention. Teach your children that it's okay to work things out for themselves, but it is also good to know when to ask for help.

Be their defender when necessary. But don't undermine the authority of the teacher by defending them when they are clearly in the wrong.

Listen to them without judgment and be fully engaged in conversation. Let them be honest about their feelings. Rather than say, "You shouldn't feel that way," maybe say, "I am sorry you are feeling..." sad, mad, unloved, overlooked, left out, or whatever the emotion of that day happens to be. Talk through the situation that invoked those feelings without judgment. If you tell them they 'shouldn't' feel a certain way, they may be reluctant to share it with you next time because they are 'wrong' or 'in trouble' simply for feeling the way they feel. Allow them to 'confess' if they need to without exhibiting too much of your own emotion. Be quick to listen, slow to speak, and slow to become angry.

Be honest with them. One student became discouraged because her parents frequently used her size as the reason she could not play a musical instrument, pursue a career in physical therapy, drive, or play a sport. The reality was that the family budget would not allow for these activities. She was led to believe her stature made her less capable. If a child cannot participate in a sport or activity because of financial, social, or other limitations, gently tell them why. Don't give them an excuse that puts the responsibility back on them for something beyond their control.

Be careful with labels. Sometimes, parents or teachers will throw around labels like "gifted," "ADD," "special," "OCD," or others. In the academic world, those labels are sometimes necessary to acquire services or help a child requires. However, a child shouldn't hear those labels bandied about as excuses or currency for a lack of responsibility or achievement. Labels should never be mentioned in front of other students. They should only be used if they have been confirmed by a professional with accompanying recommendations for steps to success as a student and as a human being. I would even argue that the student does not need to know about them until a time when they are mature enough not to take on the label as their identity.

Teach your children that we should not be a product of technology, but it should be a tool we use for the cor-

rect purposes. We need to guard our children's hearts by guarding their access to TV, computers, and social media. I would not advocate completely shutting off access because they need to learn how to live in the age of technology, but we need to teach our children how to use these tools properly, understanding the power, danger, and limitations they possess.

3. It's Not Too Late

I wish there was a rewind button for all of us who didn't have the right tools to build authentic confidence in our children as they were growing up. I tried to use the tools I have outlined above in my classroom and in raising my children. I think I raised relatively confident children, but I know I made mistakes. I lost my temper. My expectations may have been a bit unreasonable at times. And... I have had to apologize. I apologized as they were growing up when I made mistakes. I apologize now for my mistakes. And to my adult children, I have apologized for the real and perceived mistakes I made when they were children.

It's hard to put into practice what we may not have observed in our own homes and classrooms growing up. But by God's grace we can train ourselves to be the grownups we wish would have poured into our lives when we were young.

It's not too late to acknowledge your children's gifts, accomplishments, and successes. Start by praying for wisdom to see your children through the eyes of their Creator. Pray that God will give you the words to build up and not tear down.

4. *Results Of Having Authentic Confidence*

A wise master teacher once told me, "Once students realize success is within their control, the sky's the limit!" Along the path to achievement, every individual either learns authentic confidence or becomes intimidated. False confidence and being timid can be a very dangerous state of mind! We want our surgeons to be confident in their skills and training as they take a scalpel to a patient. It could be a life and death situation if they waver. The same is true for airline pilots and the other drivers on the road beside us. The reality is that authentic confidence comes from recognizing our gifts, using them, and practicing over and over. It can make us better at whatever we do. Building that kind of confidence in your child takes having a plan, patience, practice, and prayer.

If your child tries things, they will learn things. If they repeat it, they will build confidence. If they fail, they will grow. If they succeed, they will flourish. If they do nothing, they will stagnate. Authentic confidence gives individuals the ability to take healthy risks, make wise decisions, and encourage others to do the same.

Seeing your children set a goal, reach it, and be satisfied with a job well done is a great reward for a parent. The result of building authentic confidence in your child is having competent and confident adults who will be participating, contributing members of society.

Through prayer and careful coaching, that timid twenty-eight-year-old version of me learned to set goals, plan a way to meet those goals, celebrate when I reached them and clearly articulate how I got there. Believing I was created for a good purpose and valued by the One who made me unique and capable in the way I was created to be was life-changing.

Begin now. Give your children the gift of believing in the potential of who they were created to be.

Next Steps:

- Catch your child doing something good and acknowledge it.
- Tell them what to do, not always what not to do: Say, "Please Walk," rather than, "Stop running."
- Discipline in love, and if you blow it, apologize. Recovering from our real or perceived failures builds our own confidence and will yield bountiful results in relationships with our children.
- Introduce them to God and help them find their confidence in Him.
- Participate in your child's classroom, encouraging them, the other students, and the teacher.
- Pray with your kids before school and before bed, two of the most stressful times of the day. A wise parent once told me, "Prayer helps your child persevere, get through struggles, and rise above challenges. Adding prayer into their toolkit helps the child of God overcome fears, build character, and strengthen relationships."
  Pray for wisdom. (James 1:5)

- Take a hike. With your child, plan out what you will need for the adventure. Involve them in packing a picnic and allow them to carry a bit in their own backpack. While on the hike, observe and appreciate the uniqueness of every tree, cloud, bird, or other

child. Help them see and appreciate their uniqueness by helping them to see the variety in God's creation.
- Take an inventory of your child's interests, skills, talents, and gifts. If they are old enough, discuss different activities to try and how to make that happen.
- Sit down at the beginning of the school year and discuss what your child wants to accomplish and how you can make that happen together. Also, discuss your collective goals and make your expectations clear. Plan how you will celebrate the successes and intervene with course correction when needed.
- Have daily, weekly, or monthly check-ins with your child on how they are doing on their goals. Find out where they may need additional help or guidance.

  *Encourage setting goals, studying hard, and finding the right school or training programs.
- Start today practicing some of these tips to build authentic confidence in your children!

For further reading:

De Neve, Cyndie Claypool. *God-Confident Kids: Helping Your Child Find True Purpose, Passion, and Peace.* Harvest House Publishers, 2018.

Romans 5:1-5

Proverbs 3:26

Jeremiah 17:7

2 Corinthians 3:4-5

Colossians 3:21

Zephaniah 3:17

———*———

Chapter 3

Entering the College Drop-Off Zone and Empty Nest: What's a Mom to Do?

By Anna Dabill

"When I get old, I am going to be a bird and fly away." This was such a profound statement from my 4-year-old that I will always remember.

I gave one last long, tight hug, said, "I love you," and waved goodbye from the car. I got choked up, and the tears started to roll down my face. This was my first born out of three kids. I was saying goodbye to her. She was stepping out on her own to start college the next day.

On the ride home, I thought of all the years I had my kids at home and how I prepared them to fly away. The memories of time with them flooded my mind. *They are on their own. Until…they need money, have a problem they can't figure out, or come home to live on break.*

We do everything from birth to 18 to prepare for the day they leave home and begin life on their own. Not every student goes to college. Some may live at home and choose the local community college or a job to save money. A few students may choose a GAP year before starting college. (GAP Year- a year taken off by students before college.) Some parents may only experience a gradual change in the home front. The number of high school students entering college has declined since the pandemic. The U.S. Bureau of Labor and Statistics reported that in October of 2023, 61% of High School seniors moved on to college[5]. Whatever your student decides to do with your guidance will be his or her decision.

We all have different personality bents and skills, and we truly hope students move to the education or a career they enjoy. For some kids, deciding what to do for the rest of their lives is difficult. They are just learning who they are and what they like. It may take some time, wrong turns, and going back to the drawing board to figure out life. Most adults don't even know what they want to do. The research.com website from June 2024 says an average of 71% of college freshmen students will continue college in their sophomore year.[6] Don't be surprised if your student changes his or her mind now or in the future. You will learn to be flexible in this new learning curve you will soon enter.

August and September are the months we need to say goodbye to our college kids. As the college drop-off took place with two of our kids, I was thinking, "Yippy Yay!" Two fewer people in the house for whom to buy groceries and

---

[5]   U.S. Bureau of Labor Statistics. "61.8 Percent of Recent High School Graduates Enrolled in College in October 2021." *The Editor's Desk*, 17 Aug. 2022, www.bls.gov/opub/ted/2022/61-8-percent-of-recent-high-school-graduates-enrolled-in-college-in-october-2021.htm. Accessed 1 August 2024.

[6]   "College Dropout Rates." *Research.com*, 2024, www.research.com/universities-colleges/college-dropout-rates#:~:text=What%20is%20the%20average%20retention,into%20the%20next%20academic%20year. Accessed 1 August 2024.

coordinate schedules. Although I missed my girls, we often needed freedom and space from each other after summer. Even though you drop them off at school, they come home for weekends, breaks, and summer. Consider the rest of the chapter your giant to-do list mentally, physically, and spiritually for preparing your student and yourself for the college drop-off and the future empty nest.

Planning for the College Drop-Off

For some of you, this is your first student in college or your student's first year away from home. Or, it's coming in the next few years. You may be thinking how do I handle it? Here are some ideas and tips to help you in the transition from home to college.

My first tip is to think of all the life skills you want your student to know before they head to school. I think most life skills are gradually learned as we prepare for them to leave. For example, if your student didn't learn good driving skills at age 16, then focus on that.

Communication skills are essential, especially if your student does not like to communicate. This will include making their own appointments with the dentist and doctor and talking to office personnel and professors they will meet on campus. My son is introverted. The good news is that the older he gets, the better he gets at communication. At age 23, he just told me he read Dale Carnegie's book, *How to Make Friends and Influence People*.[7] "It works, Mom", he said. "I used it at an interview last week." He hated talking to

---

[7] Carnegie, Dale. *How to Win Friends and Influence People*. Simon and Schuster, 1981.

people and he dreaded this at his graduation party.

The following is what I have always told him: When someone asks you a question, answer it and either ask the same question back, if applicable or ask them an open-ended question. This way you don't have to talk as much and if they are talkers like me, they may run with the conversation. Communication is a tennis match. If you don't ask them a question, they may just keep asking you questions.

Your student should also know how to get along with other people who may be the opposite of them. Let's face it. Everyone is not like them. Your student may shine at this because of family. For others, this is something to be worked on, especially if they are set in their ways and are the only child. The college roommate experience is definitely telling of how they get along with others. Prepare him or her for living with new people and thinking of others.

Cooking skills are essential, especially if they are not on a 100% meal plan on campus or if they are living in an apartment. If you did not teach your kids all of your cooking skills, then make it your goal. Weekend food may be all they need. Then, microwave cooking recipes are easy. Some dorm rooms have kitchens you can also use, but storing all the ingredients in your little room is difficult for space.

As a Registered Dietitian, I would stress easy and healthy meals. Foods they can pack to take for lunch if living off campus, and meals they can make on the weekend or reheat throughout a busy week. One of my daughters, who lived in her own apartment, made chili, eggs, burritos, sandwiches, pasta, salad, and a cold quinoa salad. She ate many meals of those foods during a given week. Teach your kids about healthy, reasonably priced food choices when cooking on their own.

Laundry skills are important for your student to do on their own. There are the parents who have students do their own laundry at age ten and up, and it's on them. I loved doing my kids' laundry. It felt like I accomplished something as I prayed for them as I folded their clothes. My kids did have a laundry assignment in 7th grade FACS class. They were given a checklist of items by their teacher. I was supposed to teach about laundry. This involved sorting loads, soap, and water temperature. They did their required loads of laundry and passed. To get them back into the practice of laundry before leaving for college, I had them do their laundry the last six months they lived at home. If the summer was busy, I let them hand laundry back to me until they moved out. Do what is best for your family and kids, but give them lessons or a quick review. When I was In college, I overloaded the washing machine to save money, broke the dorm washer, and ended up loving to wash clothes. It all works itself out.

Finance skills are continuously learned throughout life. Students learn finances with the money they get from their summer jobs or the school year. Teach your student the power of saving, spending, and tithing with their money.

One of my daughters had a job during the school year from age 15-18. She worked part-time and loved to spend, but we had her save money. She saved and saved. When it was time to go to college, my husband looked at the first-semester bill and had her use her saved money to pay for it. Just like that it was all gone. There was about $500 left to spend. She was horrified.

"It's all gone," she said.

"Yes," we said, "and it will be our turn to pay your spring semester bill."

We told her she could get a job at school if she needed more money. She immediately found a job on campus in the first month and always had one or two part-time jobs as she went to college. Here's the good part. When she graduated, she said that was the best thing we could have ever done for her because she graduated debt-free.

Getting Ready

The first tip is to make sure the shopping is completed early and not delayed until the last minute. Make a list with your college student and start shopping in the summer to make it a fun experience. Remember that everything doesn't have to be new, especially if he or she is moving into an apartment. We loved searching for items at garage sales all summer. If you do buy something, let them buy it from their earned money so they will not get lazy when moving out and just throw it away. What will they need in the dorm or for the apartment? At the end of the section, I will include a list of recommended items to buy and bring to college.

Have your student pack the vehicle with all their supplies the night before leaving. They will realize how much they are bringing and may remember something they forgot. My husband helped our kids carry the refrigerator and heavy boxes to the car. When I moved to college, I had to unpack by myself and pack for the return home. I laugh now because my mom would send my dad to help me at college drop-off.

Dad would help by carrying the pillows and then sit by the truck and tell me, "I have bad knees. I'll make sure no one steals anything." I carried my stuff to my room. Every year, I took less and less after figuring out what was necessary and what was not.

Pray for your student the night before you leave or in the morning. This will calm nerves and let them know you will always be praying for them. The night before our daughter left for school, she had a meltdown about going to college. We said she could unpack and go to college in our town. It definitely wasn't the choice she wanted to make. Keep in mind your kids are emotional, too, and need to process all the changes related to moving away from home.

Have a heart-to-heart talk with your student while planning and packing. I wish I had gotten a little deeper with each of my kids by asking them about their fears, hopes, expectations, and anything going on in their heads.

The College Drop-Off Zone

On move-in day, you may find a group at the college that will help move the boxes and bags to the room. Some colleges do this to make freshman move-in day go more quickly and easily for parking. If you can bring siblings, mom, and dad. You will get done in no time. Dads and brothers are good at rearranging beds, adjusting loft and bunk beds, and setting up techy stuff. It's all hands on deck to get the room or apartment set up.

Plan on a trip to the store in the college town to get the items you forgot or didn't anticipate. It's the last shopping trip together, and you can then plan on eating a quick meal together on campus or at a restaurant before you say good-bye.

We all ate lunch together in the college dining center for a fun memory. Stories were told about the food we ate at the campus dining center when my husband and I went to college. Later, one of my girls complained about the food in the dining center. I said, "You have so many choices. What is to complain about?"

She said, "Mom, they make family day and move-in day food the best with all options. Other days, those choices are not there anymore." That was the case at her school. The food was excellent at our Alma Mater and at the college where our son completed his first year. Dietitians ran the food service and it was a major at the school.

Don't feel bad if your student doesn't call or text very often. Remind them to text or call you at least once a week to confirm they are alive or doing okay. One of my daughters barely calls and hates to text as an adult to this day. I know she is alive when she is on social media, or I text and ask how she is doing. I usually get the answer, "Good," to all my questions. Know your student, and don't set your expectations too high. It's a busy time of life. If you have a student who will call or text you every few days, then I cheer you on, Mom. My kids are very independent. It's good and bad at the same time.

Your kids will come home in 1-6 weeks to get more things or eat your home-cooked meals if you are within driving distance. I was shocked when one of my girls was home from school in two weeks for Labor Day weekend. She surprised us. My kids had no car, but finding a ride wasn't too hard with other students in the same school and hometown. Give them money to help pay the driver for gas on their way home. If they have a car, that is another level of responsibility.

Dear moms, this is a new season in life. Pray, pray, pray. When they are in school, you need to keep the lines of communication in place and pray for them. Text your kids or call them and ask for prayer requests. From when my youngest was in kindergarten to his senior year in high school, I led a Mom's in Prayer group each week where we prayed for our kids, each other's kids, their teachers, and their school. As my kids entered college, I kept praying for them in our Moms in Prayer group. It's like dropping your backpack of bricks off in the center of the group. We prayed for our kids, and when we left, it felt like an empty backpack. We gave our kids to God to care for their needs, teach them, and grow them away from home. Throughout the week, we kept adding bricks to our backpacks, and our group kept praying for our kids together.

Tips for Mom and Dad

- Don't bug your students every day about everything. Let them make their own decisions and give them advice when they ask for it.
- Pray and ask for prayer requests.
- Enjoy your freedom because they will be home at Thanksgiving, Christmas, Easter, Spring break, and Summer unless they go to a school that is more than driving distance.
- Figure out financial bills and who will pay them if you are helping your student through school. We have access to our kids' online checking accounts so we

can transfer money and help pay some expenses.

- Plan to visit them 6-8 weeks from the start of school and take them out to eat. If they live far away, maybe you can visit them at least one time during their college year.
- Make their favorite food when they come home. They will compliment and thank you for your cooking. After being away from home, my kids now like my food.
- Send a text of encouragement or Bible verse each week. Tell them you are praying for them.
- Encourage them to find a small group/Bible study or church so they can connect with other students and stay grounded.
- Encourage them to find a small job on campus for 4-8 hours a week to help with their resume, earn some extra cash, and keep them on a schedule.
- Send them a box of snacks via Amazon Pantry around midterms or finals. They will love it.

"Pray continually."
1 Thessalonians 5:17

Here is a quick list of items to bring to school and shop for:

- Refrigerator (unless roommate is bringing).
- Snacks, vitamins/medicines, and enough personal hygiene until the next break.
- School supplies, Kleenex, garbage bags, 3M command hooks in a variety of sizes, bath and hand towels, washcloths, bedding to fit XL twin and a cushy mattress cover, mattress pad, and pillows.
- Some of these will be specific to your students'

needs- Rugs, a comfortable fold-up chair, water bottles, cups, and a Keurig or electric tea kettle for hot water, tea, or coffee. Laundry supplies, a laundry bag, a large plastic bin to store extra supplies, extension cords/surge protector, a wifi modem (if not supplied), and a fan if there is no air conditioning.

- A container to put bathroom supplies in if they don't have a bathroom in their room.
- In-season clothing for the semester. Return out-of-season clothes for the next semester.
- Decorations, especially for girls. Make it simple and buy a fabric tapestry you can put on the wall with velcro command strips. My daughter loved her tapestry and put it in her room at home in the summer.
- Furniture and home goods if your student is living in an apartment. Shop during the summer for pots and pans, kitchen goods, dishes, vacuums, lamps, and furniture at thrift stores and garage sales. Remember to buy Kleenex, paper towels, dish and hand soap, garbage bags, toilet paper, cleaning supplies, dishcloths/ towels, and food.

The Empty Nest. What's a Mom to do?

This little nest has been a busy nest for the past 22 years. One kid, two kids, then three kids in our nest. Activities of feeding, teaching these little birds to fly, and all the other life lessons. One by one, the kids each took their turn and left the nest. Now, I have an "Empty Nest," so what's mama to do? When my youngest started college, I was looking at the straw in my nest. No more birds to feed each day or show them the way. If I did any parenting of my lovely kids, it would be from a distance, by text, phone, or when they come home on break.

When my youngest was born, I remember thinking about my age. *When he turns 18 and graduates from high school, I will be 50 years old.* That memory was so vivid as I thought about it, and now we are both past that age. Time moves on.

I remember when my youngest was four years old, he was staring out the patio door, and looking outside. I asked him, "What are you looking at?" He looked at me and said, "When I get old, I am going to be a bird and fly away."

I smiled and said, "Yes, you will." I was so amazed my 4-year-old said this that I immediately wrote it down so I could treasure these words.

What he said is true. He graduated high school with an AA degree and headed to college in the fall. He grew up and learned how to take care of those wings. He is still learning where those wings will take him. Not everything goes as planned. After one semester of college, COVID-19 hit, and many kids looked at their majors and life and asked, "Is this for me?" In my son's case, he didn't like his major and decided to take some time off to work. Living on his own, he started school again part-time while working part-time. The light is coming, and he plans to graduate debt-free in 2025.

Some birds take a little coaching along the way. As mamas, we will still be coaching the college and adult kids. The "nest time" with Mom and Dad goes fast. The little birds have grown and are on their own.

What's a mama bird to do with her life? That was my question for the past five years. I am always asking God to tell me what is next. My motto has been the "next right thing."

So what did I do? I started a blog in 2018. This chapter and my dream to publish my picture book have been my "next right thing." I am working on a few picture books and working part-time as a dietitian. In 2020, my husband and I sold our house, quit our jobs, and planned to take a traveling sabbatical. We traveled the middle states, hiking and biking and meeting people with stories. We wanted to see the USA and figure out where we needed to live next and what God wanted us to do. We had planned to do this after our last kid left for college. By March, Covid hit, and we completed our travels in May. We lived with relatives waiting on God's next right thing.

Eventually, with God's perfect timing, we ended up with jobs and living on the East Coast, 1,200 miles from our family. Our kids were on their own and grown, and we had started our own new life. We put on our wings and flew away from our original nest to start a new one. It was a midlife change or alteration we needed. The majority of my life revolved around the nest. I had spent many years pouring into my kids, nurturing them, teaching them life skills, praying for them, and helping them grow.

These moments have passed by. My nest is empty but still open to new possibilities every single year.

What's next for you?

Speaking from my experience, I suggest you do a little tidying or cleaning of the nest. A little decluttering and saying goodbye to the things you don't need that complicate your life. I sorted things we wanted to give to our kids and things we didn't need. I sold things at garage sales, Marketplace, or made donations.

Sometimes, it's obvious what you will do when the kids leave because you talk about it all the time. Other times, it's not. My husband had a dream of moving when the last kid graduated from school. He and I wanted to move someplace warmer than Minnesota with new adventures. It may be clear what you need to do because of your past experiences, your likes, personality, gifts, and talents. Deep inside, you will know which direction to head. It's a great time to try new things and see if you like them. You don't have to have all the answers now; after all, your kids are learning this too.

This almost empty nest nearly isn't that bad, when you think of the freedom it gives in the future. You can find new jobs and new possibilities. You will always love your kids and stay connected with them. An almost empty nest can be a good thing. Just smile when you realize the time is winding down and things will change.

Empty Nest To-Do List

1. Pray for your kids. Pray they will continue to grow in their faith, knowledge, and relationships and communicate with you.

2. Pray for what God wants you to do with your new time and maybe even your place and space.

3. Enjoy all the new freedom you will have now.

4. Discover who you are again without connection to your kids. Note: It is harder to make new friends when you don't have kids to naturally introduce you to other

moms.

5. Communicate with your independent kids and enjoy the new life they will bring to you.

6. Grow in new ways: Connection with God, husband, church, hobbies, or job.

7. Set some new goals for your future.

8. Spend time with people. If your kids kept you from building relationships with family or friends, then this is your opportunity.

9. Listen to God, your kids, your husband, and others. Just listen, don't talk!

Dear Mom, continue to pray and prepare your student and yourself for the college drop-off and the empty nest. The day your kids leave home and fly away will happen sooner than you think. Make a list of what you want to do when the kids leave, and dream about it for a bit. Finally, make a list of what needs to happen to prepare your kids for the college drop-off.

I will leave you with a quote from a children's book I loved as a kid by P.D. Eastman titled The Best Nest.[8] If you haven't said this before your kids leave, you will most definitely say this when they come home for a visit. Even if you move to a new state like me, you will still say this because parenting is all about the heart of your family and being together. "I love my Nest. In all the world my nest is best."

---

8 Eastman, P.D. The Best Nest. Random House, 1968.

Chapter 4

———✳———

Joy for the Journey, Wisdom for the Way: A Mother's Reflections on Trust, Growth, and God's Guidance

By: Kayren J. Cathcart

"TRUST IN THE LORD WITH ALL THINE HEART; AND LEAN NOT UNTO THINE OWN UNDERSTANDING.
IN ALL THY WAYS ACKNOWLEDGE HIM,
AND HE SHALL DIRECT THY PATHS."
PROVERBS 3:5-6, KJV

My two children are in college and recently got their driver's licenses. We've celebrated many milestones throughout their lives, but none as momentous as The Great 2nd Grade Science Fair Project fiasco.

I thought I'd "graduated" when I survived The Great Play-Doh Turtle-in-a-Shoebox Animal Habitat Project with my mind intact. What teacher gives kindergartners projects anyway? Apparently, the teachers of my children. So, I should have been prepared for another science project by second grade, right? *Wrong.*

A little background: Throughout my tenure as a grade school student, science fair projects (gulp) were my absolute **bane**. Make no mistake, I could do them. It was just *the process* that I disdained immensely. Why? Because it challenged my time management abilities and caused me to plan *and execute*. I was great at the planning but sloppy in my execution, which usually entailed waiting until the last minute. I wondered, "What exactly does this have to do with real life anyway? I'm a literary person, so why do I have to deal with this science stuff every new school year?"

As the adult in the room, I realized I was going to have to face this phobia with my kids. And not just deal with it but *conquer it* boldly. After weeks and months of agonizing, planning, preparing, and executing, we concluded the experiment, finished the research paper, printed the hypothesis, cut out graphics, and pasted until our hearts were content. Not only did I survive, but I emerged from the process stronger than I expected. I was *super* glad when it was done (trust me!), but emerged with a greater appreciation for why God made me face my own science project angst and trepidation head-on.

I've learned that God equips us to handle whatever need arises and teaches us to trust His faithfulness. I was facing my fears at the time, but I now see the joy in that part of the journey. Survival gives one a great appreciation for challenge, eh?

God showed me many things through working with my child on this project, including how very alike we are, in more ways than I care to admit. These included:

- Sometimes being bright with natural aptitude = wanting to rush through the process
- Our inclination to take the path of least resistance = being more focused on reaching the destination than enjoying the journey
- Our intense, perfectionist, self-critical tendencies= not being patient with the process and sometimes getting unduly frustrated with the little things.

I had plenty of opportunities for teachable moments – as a teacher *and* a student. For example, I overcame the urge to finish the report myself just so it would be done – because I'd be robbing my child of the learning process.

Bottom Line Praise Report: My child was selected as one of the top three 2nd Graders to advance a project to the school's science fair! My initial goal had been simply to "get it done and turn it in." Sad to admit, but I wasn't aiming for excellence. "Pretty good" would've been just fine with me. But my child saw the guidelines for a great project, and he really wanted to win. Since we serve a God of excellence and not mediocrity, I had to practice what I preach and give my best effort. After all of my foot-dragging, complaining about how I didn't want to do this because it's just one more thing on my already full plate, yada yada yada...God showed that **He** was in the midst of the whole thing.

So it really was never about me at all. It never is! It's al_ways for God's purposes. And this time, I believe God wanted to see a snaggle-toothed smile from a boy who won a prize full of science gold, complete with modeling clay, a slinky, a microscope, and whatever else was in that package. He had his moment in the spotlight – being featured on the morning announcements, receiving congratulatory cheers from his classmates, standing on the stage beaming in front of peers and parents, and getting his picture taken by his little sister, who was genuinely proud of him.

Did he win first place in the school science fair? Nope – not even second or third place. But in our eyes, he stood head and shoulders above the competition, including 3rd through 5th graders. He represented us well, and our whole family was there to support him for his hard work and to celebrate his accomplishments. We have the certificates to prove it and that big tri-fold board that I still haven't forgotten over a decade later, even as we approach his college graduation.

I continue to be overwhelmed with God's miraculous love that gives mothers such a tremendous job. More amazing is that the assignment is given along with His promise to never leave nor forsake us, and His promise to provide the wisdom and guidance we need daily. How comforting to know that we're never alone as we face the challenges and joys of motherhood! We can trust God to direct our paths – even into a new school year.

Hey Mama, I know it's tough to navigate the transition from summer (moment of silence...sigh) into a new school year, no matter what stage your child is in. Despite all my incessant ranting, raving, and cajoling to "Take your baths... put your laundry in the hamper...brush your teeth...put Vaseline on your lips...turn the light out," I've done it myself for 12+ years – twice! As my children are both in college now, I reflect on how I've grown right alongside them with each opportunity for a fresh start. I've learned to treat moments as miracles instead of stressing over insignificant stuff. Determining significance in light of eternity can work wonders for putting things into proper perspective - in the blink of an eye. **Reflect, reset/rest, reignite!**

Your "momming" may not look like someone else's, but that's okay – you're getting the job done. From this vantage point, I can encourage you that you're doing great!

No matter how many times other people said it, I had to learn to internalize this message for myself. Sometimes, we take ourselves way too seriously! There's no template for this work, and we learn as we go. However, that is why we raise our children – so they can grow, develop, mature, and become equipped to face life confidently with the lessons we've instilled in them.

Reflect

As your child grows through this school year, you will grow also, my friend. I encourage you to prayerfully prepare for the back-to-school season. Also, remove the "pressure to perform" or to be "perfect," trust God, and enjoy the journey as you and your children mature. If this OCD helicopter mom survived 12 years of school with two children and we're halfway through college, there's hope for you as well!

> *"Do not be anxious or worried about anything, but in everything [every circumstance and situation] by prayer and petition with thanksgiving, continue to make your [specific] requests known to God."*
> Philippians 4:6, AMP

I can tell you that not stressing about the details of ev-ery. little. thing. is within your reach as you see gifts of joy tucked into the mundane moments of each day. I Peter 5:7 reminds us to cast **all** our cares, anxieties, worries, and con-cerns on God because He cares for us. If I could find joy in facing yet *another* science fair project (literally every school year, they were my bane!), you can begin to anticipate joy for this school year with your children – with God's help! We are not alone in this big job on our plates – thank goodness!

> *"Commit thy way unto the Lord; trust also in him;*
> *and he shall bring it to pass."*
> Psalm 37:5, KJV

Rest and Reset

Ok, friend...do you ever find yourself doing way too much and realizing you need to cut out or at least pause some things, just for sanity's sake? If so, I believe this means it's time for us to evaluate (or reevaluate) our priorities. Some-times, the people, places, things, experiences, memories, hopes, or even dreams we once held close no longer align with where we are in the present, especially as moms. When this occurs and manifests itself in an overstuffed schedule, reduced productivity, or unrealistic expectations, it's time to make some adjustments.

I can attest to being the first partaker of this message!

Over the past several months, several wake-up calls have underscored my finite capacity and helpless inability to whip out the invisible Wonder Woman cape and boots from the back of the closet at a second's notice. Not that I didn't realize I had limitations. Trust me, I am aware of my personal limitations! But in trying not to focus on them, I blurred the lines between fantasy and reality. I didn't notice that I'd been slowly but steadily creeping back to attempting to save the world in my own strength – again. My sheer exhaustion and utter fatigue should've tipped me off. Proverbs 3:5-6 is a real anchor when the overwhelm of life threatens. Relief came with acknowledging that I was unable to **1)** clone myself, or **2)** be in two different places at the same time.

Let's free ourselves this new school year from the "What will people say?" mindset. Commit to "Stop doing crazy." Fight that random, bizarre pop-up thought that may be residue from PPD (People-Pleasing Disorder) or CHD (Chronic Helping Disorder) that still lingers, no matter how hard you've scrubbed. As long as we're doing our best to walk in excellence according to God's Word and not minimizing or excluding this as a priority, we can breathe a sigh of relief, rest in the Lord, and release ourselves from unrealistic expectations (whether real or, most likely, perceived). The book of Matthew gives us an excellent reminder:

"Come unto me, all ye that labour and are heavy laden, and I will give you rest. Take my yoke upon you, and learn of me; for I am meek and lowly in heart: and ye shall find rest unto your souls. For my yoke is easy, and my burden is light." Matthew 11:28-30, KJV

You are enough because you're connected to the One Who is *more* than enough. His grace is sufficient for you. And it's not all on you either. Having a support system makes all the difference in the world. Moms often overlook this fact until approaching burnout. It's imperative to take preventive measures that reduce stress so you can bask in the joy that's embedded in this journey called family. You can do this! Paul reminds us where our sufficiency comes from in 2 Corinthians:

"Such is the confidence and steadfast reliance and absolute trust that we have through Christ toward God. Not that we are sufficiently qualified in ourselves to claim anything as coming from us, but our sufficiency and qualifications come from God." 2 Corinthians 3:4-5, AMP

Seriously, there are *lots* of distractions vying for our attention. Here are a few of my favorite questions to ask myself when overwhelm tries to creep in and do a hostile takeover:

1. What's my goal?
2. Is this activity going to help me move closer to that goal?
3. If I say "yes" to this, what am I saying "no" to?

Sometimes, we've got to slow down long enough to think about what that next step will look like, and then prepare to take it! This is the value of taking time to reset as we approach the new school year.

Reignite!

As mothers, sometimes we don't give ourselves enough credit for the work we've done, the tests we've passed, or the challenges we've overcome. Let reflection propel you forward and reignite your passion for what's to come in the new school year.

I remember the journaling iterations that took me through a "sticker season." Creative expression through art can be quite cathartic and therapeutic. A "glitter gel pen season," where I'd write in a different color on each line (oooh, pretty sparkles!), and my "black and white season," where I only wrote in black ink to stay focused while writing in my black and white journal. I was seeking clarity in several areas of my life, and it came.

Though I used to drag my feet in resistance to change, I now look forward to the newness of what's to come. Last year, my transition into a new school year precipitated The Embracing Change Chronicles when I went from redhead to brunette in 30 minutes flat. It wasn't just hair color. It was a confidence-boosting transformation.

When I walked into my appointment, I didn't ask to see the color she'd selected due to a mild in-car panic attack that "light brown can mean a range of different colors on the spectrum, so I wonder where she stands." I said, "I'm ready; let's color!" and I didn't even try to peek while the color was processing. I relaxed and enjoyed my "me-time" under the cool mist steamer. My hairdresser knows me, my personality, my likes and dislikes. She's supported me through *many* life transitions, so I trust her.

This was a bigger event than simply changing my hair color. The process was an outward manifestation of a mindset transition that had been in the making for months (Ok, years). I'm getting the hang of embracing change and finally learning to "just roll with it." You will, too! *#ProgressIsAProcess*

As mothers, we sometimes forget to allow ourselves time to be rewarded for the many sacrifices we make on a daily basis. But when we remember, it helps us to keep our serving and caring for others in perspective. All giving without being replenished and restored leads to imbalance. Yet, an occasional splurge doesn't hurt. As a matter of fact, it helps. When we feel relaxed, appreciated, and renewed, there's no end to the benefits our families reap. On the flip side, we all know what pent-up resentment coupled with overtiredness and frazzled feelings lead to...and that untimely explosion ain't pretty! Remember, self-care is not selfish. It's a gift you deserve and must intentionally incorporate into your schedule.

Conclusion

As moms, we're often too hard on ourselves. We think that if we don't do everything "just right," our children will suffer. Despite all my incessant ranting, raving, cajoling, and coaxing, "Take your baths...put your laundry in the hamper... brush your teeth...put Vaseline on your lips...turn the light out!" my children have emerged as strong, disciplined, productive members of society. What more can we ask for? With over two decades of experience and counting, I've learned that the critters are rather resilient despite my maternal imperfections. What a great God we serve!

Continue to rely on His wisdom, strength, and guidance for this next leg of the journey called motherhood. Gratefully, there are footprints to follow along this path...blessings to you for answering the call to the work and joy of motherhood!

May your back-to-school season and every day going forward be filled with the joy of the Lord, which is your strength. Do we get tired and weary sometimes? Absolutely! But we can walk in abundant blessings as we undertake every task and assignment associated with and required for building the foundation of future generations. This is no small feat, but one for which God has thoroughly equipped us with His Word and His Spirit to accomplish in excellence and for His glory. Be encouraged as you trust the Lord to guide you through every twist and turn along the journey of motherhood.

> *"For with God nothing shall be impossible. And Mary said, Behold the handmaid of the Lord; be it unto me according to thy word. And the angel departed from her."*
> Luke 1:37-38, KJV (emphasis added)

When we choose to abide (live in) the joy of the Lord, He guides our paths daily, and the "work" of family becomes delightsome. Learn to see the joy in each season of your journey and embrace the wisdom of the Word as you walk in the way God is leading you and your family.

Next Steps

In our achievement-addicted culture, we can get caught up in the misnomer that raising children is all about the outcome when truthfully, it's the *journey* that matters most. It's about the moments of joy that inhabit that journey, make for rich experiences, and create unforgettable, treasured, indelible memories. I hope this chapter has encouraged you to "zoom out" about 10,000 feet to see the bigger picture beyond the day-to-day routine of "get up, drop off, pick up, do homework, etc."

There is joy embedded in your journey – right where you are, right now. I encourage you to take inventory as you reflect, reset, and reignite for this new school year.

Reflect

- Express gratitude for what was, what is, and what is to come in the lives of your children as they embark on a new chapter in their educational adventure.
  - Choose a creative outlet of your choice for this expression (i.e., art, music, exercise, journaling, prayer) and feel the JOY!
- Acknowledge how *you* have grown over the past year.
  - Identify Three things you did well and celebrate them!

Rest and Reset

- Take a moment to pause before setting your schedule for the upcoming week.
  - Invite God to show you his wisdom for the way so you can experience the joy of this year's unique journey.
- Take an unapologetic moment for self-care.
  - Do yourself a favor and have that cup of coffee made by someone else. Take an extra 10 minutes driving home to enjoy some different scenery. Lock the door and luxuriate in that monthly (or quarterly) bubble bath. Without guilt. Because you've earned it. If your family can attest to your sacrifices (and most of them speak for them-

selves), then you more than owe it to yourself to reset and enjoy a reward from time to time.

Reignite!

- Consider what life transitions you can choose to more readily accept and embrace.

Take a moment to dream about what blessings God has in store for you and your children wrapped up in the gift of this new year...then enjoy the journey!

"She looketh well to the ways of her household, and eateth not the bread of idleness.

Her children arise up, and call her blessed: her husband also, and he praiseth her.

Many daughters have done virtuously, but thou excellest them all."

Proverbs 31:27-29 KJV

Chapter 5

---✳---

Loving Your Unique Self: Avoiding the Comparison Trap

By: Enid Meyer Tchir

"YOU MADE ALL THE DELICATE, INNER PARTS OF MY BODY AND KNIT ME TOGETHER IN MY MOTHER'S WOMB. THANK YOU FOR MAKING ME SO WONDERFULLY COMPLEX!"
PSALM 139:13-14, NLT

"Comparison is the thief of all joy" —Theodore Roosevelt

As the school year begins, the excitement and challenges of new classes, friendships, and activities can sometimes lead to an overwhelming sense of comparison. Whether you're a mom helping your pre-teen or teen navigate these waters or a student stepping into the new school year, it's crucial to remember the importance of embracing individuality. God has uniquely crafted each of us with specific gifts, talents, and purposes. In this chapter, we'll explore how to avoid the comparison trap and focus on the blessings of your unique journey. By celebrating your

God-given uniqueness, learning to rejoice in others' successes, and setting personal goals, you can confidently transition back to school together (as mom and student!), secure in the knowledge that you are wonderfully made.

Moms, I hope this chapter will inspire you to be a great listener and get creative with the practical suggestions listed here. I'm praying that we will continue to parent in a loving and compassionate way, remembering our own middle-school and high-school angst. This chapter is written not only for you as the parent but for your student, so you can hand this book to him or her and say, "I think this will really help!"

Story of Addison

Addy was entering 9th grade, and she wanted to be excited, but she felt 100% fearful instead. Her neighborhood was zoned for a public high school where she hardly knew anyone. Addy wanted to begin 9th grade at another high school a few miles away, where several of her friends from church attended. Addy's mom prayed with her about this, and they decided to write to the principal, making every effort to switch schools. Despite their pleas and prayers, the school district said no, and Addy was devastated. God, however, knew exactly what He was doing.

After crying herself to sleep for a week, Addy braced for her first day of high school. The halls were busy, and some of the teenagers towered over her. Many of the older girls wore a lot of makeup, and most seemed able to afford all the coolest clothes. It was hard not to compare herself to the other girls, but when she did, she only felt small and inadequate.

Addy missed the familiar faces from her old school and even got lost walking to class twice in one day. Soon, however, Addy became friends with a few girls who sat near her in History. One day, she joined two school clubs and made even more friends. It turned out that Addy had a sense of humor, and people thought she was funny!

Addy realized she did not have to fit in with everyone; she only had to find a small circle of friends! After praying every morning and trying to be a little bit more giving to others, Addy was surprised to find that, in just a short time, she was enjoying high school.

As 9th grade ended, Addy saw a poster that encouraged students to join the student council and run for a position for the next school year. Wait...they were looking for candidates to run for president of the upcoming 10th grade?? Could she do it? Did she dare?

Addy knew one of her God-given talents was her artistic ability, so she set out to make the most vibrant, outstanding posters that boldly claimed, "Addy for 10th grade President!" and "Add Addy to Your Ballot!"

Guess what? Not only did Addy win and become class president for the 10th-grade class, but she also did the same in the 11th and 12th grades! Most importantly, Addy never compromised her Christian convictions. She trusted God, and He led her in the direction of His plan. By graduation, Addy had a ton of friends at the very high school she had never wanted to attend.

Because of the leadership skills the Lord allowed Addy to develop, Addy began to help other teenagers become Christians and was accepted to the #1 college of her choice!

Recognize Your God-Given Uniqueness

Imagine you are a one-of-a-kind masterpiece crafted by God with special talents, gifts, and a unique purpose that no one else has. Ephesians 2:10 says, "For we are God's handiwork, created in Christ Jesus to do good works, which God prepared in advance for us to do." This means that you have been made exactly as you are for a reason, and God has amazing plans just for you! (If you don't believe me, read Jeremiah 29:11-13.)

Psalm 139 also reminds us that we are "fearfully and wonderfully made." So, instead of comparing yourself to others, celebrate your uniqueness! Embrace who you are, knowing that God has a special path laid out for you, filled with opportunities to shine in your own incredible way. In this psalm, God says He knit you together in your momma's womb...He knew exactly who He was making!

Moms and teens: Now that we've talked about how important it is to recognize your God-given uniqueness, let's dive into some practical ways to make this a daily habit. I designed these tips to help you stay positive and focused on your personal journey. By starting a gratitude journal, creating daily affirmations, and doing a fun reflection exercise with one another, you can build a strong sense of self-worth and appreciation for your unique gifts. Let's get started!

Gratitude Journal

Starting a gratitude journal is a great way to remind yourself of all the amazing qualities about you and your life. Each day, take a few minutes to write down at least three things you're grateful for. This can be anything from a talent you're proud of to a small win you had at home, work, or school. Reflecting on your strengths and achievements helps you appreciate your unique journey and keeps you focused on the positive. It's like building a collection of happy moments you can look back on whenever you need a boost!

Affirmations

Creating daily affirmations means giving yourself a little pep talk every day. Think of a few positive statements that remind you of your worth and God-given uniqueness, such as "I am fearfully and wonderfully made" or "I have unique talents that make me special." You can also say, "I am a kind and loving person," and "God loves me, and he LIKES me, too!" Say these affirmations to yourself every morning or whenever you need a confidence boost. They can help you stay grounded in who you are and keep negative comparisons at bay.

Reflection Exercise

Moms and teens: Take some time to list your unique qualities and talents—those things that make you, you! It could be anything from being a good listener to rocking at a particular sport or subject. Once you have your list, share it with one another. This can be a fun and bonding experience, helping you both see the special gifts God has given each of you. You can do this with your friends, too. Plus, it's a great reminder that everyone has their own amazing, God-given qualities worth celebrating.

Celebrate Others Without Comparing

Whether we are an adult or a student, it's so easy to feel a bit jealous when we see our friends succeed, especially in areas where perhaps we have not personally flourished. However, God calls us to "Rejoice with those who rejoice; mourn with those who mourn" (Romans 12:15, NIV). This means we should celebrate our friends' wins just as enthusiastically as we would our own. When your friend goes on a fabulous vacation, aces a test, or gets that role in the play, cheer them on! Their success doesn't take away from your own talents or achievements. Instead, it shows that there's plenty of room for everyone to shine in their unique ways.

Celebrating others without comparing ourselves can make our friendships stronger and more genuine. When we lift each other up, we create a positive and supportive environment where everyone feels valued. Remember, your friends' successes are not a reflection of *your* worth. By focusing on being happy for others, you can free yourself from the negativity of comparison and feel more secure and joyful in your journey. So next time someone you know does something great, give them a high five, send a congratulatory text, or celebrate with them. Your support will mean so much to them, and you'll feel encouraged, too!

Celebrating others' successes without comparing yourself can be challenging, but it's totally worth it! Here are some practical tips to help you create a supportive and positive environment where everyone can thrive. By encouraging peer support, role-modeling positive behavior, and focusing on uplifting conversations, you can make a big difference in your friendships and your community.

Encourage Peer Support

Encouraging peer support means being your friends' biggest cheerleader. When your friend achieves something awesome, show them how proud you are! Whether it's a handwritten card, a shout-out on social media, or a heartfelt compliment, your support can make their success even sweeter. By creating a circle of friends who lift each other up, you'll all feel more confident and happy in your own accomplishments.

Role Modeling

Moms can play a huge role in this by showing how it's done. When moms (big sisters and aunties, too) openly celebrate others in their community, it sets a great example. Whether it's congratulating a neighbor on their new job or praising a friend's achievement, this positive behavior is contagious. When teens see their moms genuinely happy for others, it encourages them to do the same and creates a culture of support and kindness.

Positive Conversations

Having positive conversations is all about focusing on growth and success together. Instead of comparing who did better on a test or who got more likes on their post, talk about what everyone is working on and what goals they're aiming for. These uplifting chats help everyone stay motivated and remind you that there's enough success to go around for everyone. By keeping the conversation positive, you help create an environment where everyone feels valued and inspired.

Focus on Your Own Growth and Goals

When it comes to achieving your best, it's all about focusing on *your* path and not getting distracted by what others are doing. The Bible encourages us in Hebrews 12:1-2 to "run with perseverance the race marked out for us, fixing our eyes on Jesus, the pioneer and perfecter of faith (NIV)."

This scripture refers to our life-long faith; it can also inspire us to set personal goals and work towards them with determination, all while keeping our eyes on what truly matters. Let's explore how focusing on your own growth can lead to amazing personal achievements and a deeper sense of fulfillment. God wants us to grow!

Goal Setting

Setting personal goals that matter to you is a great way to stay motivated and see how far you've come. Students, whether it's getting better at a subject in school, trying out a new hobby, or making new friends, strive for these goals. Moms: your goals might include creating a healthier meal plan for the family, hitting a career milestone, or carving out time for your own friendships. When you focus on your achievements, you feel more confident and less worried about comparing yourself to others. Remember, God made you the exact woman He wants you to be and has great plans just for you. Keep going, stay determined, and believe that God believes in you. All of this leads to an even bigger goal: becoming the best version of yourself so you can let your light shine for others.

Progress Tracking

Tracking your progress is a great way to stay motivated and appreciate how far you've come. Keep a journal or use an app to note your achievements and steps you've taken towards your goals. Celebrate your victories, no matter how small they seem. This not only boosts your confidence but also keeps you focused on your personal growth rather than what others are doing. Enjoy your personal race and run it with perseverance (see Hebrews 12:1-2 again).

Prayer and Meditation

Incorporating prayer and meditation into your routine can help you stay grounded and focused on your unique journey. Take time each day to pray or meditate, asking for guidance and strength to pursue your goals. This helps you stay connected to your faith and reminds you to keep your eyes on Jesus. With prayer and meditation, you can find peace and clarity, making it easier to concentrate on your growth and avoid the trap of comparison.

Conclusion

As you head into this school year, remember the key points we've discussed: recognize your God-given uniqueness, celebrate others without comparing, and focus on your own growth and goals. Each of you has special talents and a unique path laid out by God, and it's important to embrace that. By appreciating your strengths and cheering on your friends, you can create a positive and supportive environment where everyone thrives.

Moms and teens out there, always remember that you are wonderfully made by God. Your worth isn't measured by how you compare to others; God designed you to be YOU. Embrace your individuality and trust that God has an amazing plan for you. Proverbs 3:5-7 is worth memorizing, for sure! Lean on your faith and let it guide you through the ups and downs of the school year.

"Trust in the Lord with all your heart and lean not on your own understanding; in all your ways submit to him, and he will make your paths straight. Do not be wise in your own eyes; fear the Lord and shun evil" (Proverbs 3:5-7, NIV).

Let's end with a prayer: *"Dear Lord, we ask for Your strength, wisdom, and peace as we navigate this school year. Help us to remember our unique worth and to support and celebrate each other without comparison. Guide us to focus on our own growth and to trust in the special purpose You have for each of us. Amen."*

When we celebrate others without comparison and focus on our own growth, we can navigate the school year with confidence and grace. We will know that we are perfectly created by God for a special purpose.

Reflection Questions:

1. What are three unique qualities God has given you?

2. How can you celebrate a friend's success this week?

3. What is one personal goal you can set for this school year?

Next Steps:

Gratitude Journal: Start a gratitude journal today and write down three things you are thankful for each day. (Hint: It really helps to keep this next to your bed and do this every night. You'll be surprised how many blessings you want to write down!)

Affirmation Practice: Write and recite daily affirmations that reinforce your unique identity and God's plan for you. Tape them to your bathroom mirror, making them easy to recite every morning.

Goal Chart: Create a goal chart with your personal milestones for the school year and track your progress. Ask a parent to do the same and set a weekly time to share your progress.

Chapter 6

---*---

A New Chapter Begins: Balancing Joy, Fear, and Faith as Your Child Enters High School

By Nikki Tigg

GOD PROVIDES ME WITH THE GRACE TO
EMBRACE THIS SEASON OF LIFE.

ANONYMOUS

I fought back the tears as I heard the darkness say, "You won't be needed anymore."

I woke up with a mind full of racing thoughts and a heart that wanted to be joyful but was fearful instead. I started the day with a sigh, knowing that I would soon drop my son off for the first day of High School. *It's not my first day of school. Why am I the one with butterflies?*

Then, I recalled a conversation with another mom. She had a son older than mine, and we talked about how big of a step this was. I told her in a whiny and complaining voice, "I can't believe that I will drop my son off at high school tomorrow." She casually responded, "Well, it won't last long because he'll be driving before you know it, and he won't need you to drive him." Stunned by her casual and sharp response, I somehow heard, "You won't be needed anymore." This conversation with a mom who'd been in my shoes didn't pan out to be one of comfort and encouragement.

My early morning thoughts continued.
I should have prepared him better for what's ahead.
What if he starts hanging out with the wrong crowd and making poor choices?
I should have done more.
What if he gets bullied?
What if he can't balance the homework load while playing sports?
What if he gets lost?
Will he have someone to sit with during lunch?

The sound of my phone notifying me of a text message snapped me back into reality. It was a text from a wonderful woman I'd met the evening before at a football scrimmage. As we talked, I learned that she was a math teacher at the school, and she taught freshmen. I shared with her that I had an incoming freshman and, after a quick glance at his schedule, I realized she was his first-period math teacher. She shared reassuring words as I opened up to her about my nervous heart. We realized we attended the same church and had lots in common. We chatted, exchanged phone numbers, and then went our separate ways as the scrimmage ended.

The text that morning was from this wonderful teacher, who was thoughtful enough to share encouraging words with my momma heart. Her reassuring words soothed my heart in a way I didn't know I needed. I felt seen. I felt understood. I felt God caring for my anxious heart.

I desperately wanted to cling to that feeling but as we went through the morning, the feeling was harder and harder to grasp.

My son and I prayed aloud on the way to school as we'd done on the way to middle school. But that day, my overwhelmed heart needed more prayer than our short drive would allow.

We entered the school entrance, which was much larger and daunting than his middle school. Confused about which line was for drop-off, I made my way through cars after locating the correct one. We said our goodbyes, and he quickly got out of the car. He joined the army of kids flooding in for their first day.

I fought back the tears as I heard the darkness say, "You won't be needed anymore."

The wrestling of emotions continued. The tears formed, and the tears fell as I drove away, leaving my baby in a place that would have so much influence on him over the next four years. On day one, I was driving him to school but at the end of the four years here, he would be driving. He would be an adult with plans of leaving home for college.

I drove home with a mind full of thoughts and a heart full of emotions. Maybe you can relate. You may feel grief that your baby is growing up, yet gratitude that you're able to offer support during this transition. Your heart may feel tender with thoughts of how your role as a parent will shift over the coming years, yet you may have a sense of excitement for what's to come. My emotions ranged from feeling thankful to have a son who does well in school to feeling proud that he's growing up while also being sad that he's growing up. My mind was also simultaneously wondering how we got here so quickly because it felt like kindergarten drop-off was only a couple of years ago.

The first several days and weeks were tough, and I knew I couldn't allow my worries to continue to cripple me. I decided that instead of being worried about that big, new school and all the "bad influences," I would pray. I told a few other moms about the tug on my heart to pray and organized a group of moms to prayer-walk the school grounds weekly. We prayed for everyone from faculty, students, and parents to bus drivers and janitors. I truly believe that was the turning point for me, and being the mom of a high school student began to feel more like a welcomed friend instead of a suspicious stranger. My prayers began to shape my thoughts about the school and my son's experience. I told myself a different story and reframed how I viewed my season of life. I developed a new perspective and told myself things like,

"It's not that I won't be needed anymore, but I get to be present and help guide him through the highs and lows of High School."

"I'm excited for him to grow up and go into the world because the world needs what he has."

"High school is a natural next step for him. Why would I be so fearful?"

"He will be a light shining in the dark places."

"He may be out of my reach, but he's still in God's hand."

"I believe he will choose friends who have a pure heart and pursue righteousness and peace."

I felt empowered to embrace this season of life; it was as if I found a freedom that seemed to be hidden before. My journey to this new mindset wasn't one I drifted to but one of deliberation. It came from being honest about my feelings, surrendering them to God, and replacing the whispers of darkness with shouts of Light.

As you navigate this season of parenting, you can feel empowered to embrace the highs, lows, and everything in between while identifying and honoring your own emotions.

Reveal what you feel.

Much like a rollercoaster, the emotions felt in this season can have sudden highs, lows, twists, and turns that can range anywhere from feelings of sadness to joy, stress, or excitement. We tend to share and show feelings of joy and excitement the most, but what about the less desirable feelings of overwhelm, anxiety, loneliness, or fear? Those feelings were the hardest for me to accept and voice, but revealing and admitting my feelings was the first step to riding the wave of emotions.

What do you do with the emotions that feel heavy, complicated, and hard to understand? You name them and refuse to ignore them because, like a beach ball trying to be held underwater, they will always appear no matter how hard you struggle to keep them concealed. This can be tough for moms because we tend to give in to the notion that we need to "have it all together" and ignore our feelings in an effort to keep others happy. Dear momma, wherever you are right now, take a breath, then take a longer, deeper one. You are not a robot, void of feelings. Your feelings aren't bad, scary, too big, or unwelcome. You don't have to suppress your feelings about this stage of motherhood to protect your child. Reject the notion that you have to hide how you feel.

Admitting how I felt in that season of motherhood was uncomfortable but liberating. Revealing your emotions is critical and will require vulnerability and extreme honesty. It won't be comfortable, but it's necessary to reveal your emotions to honor them.

No matter how uncomfortable, take a moment to check in with yourself and see how you are truly feeling. It's also possible that you don't even know what you're feeling.

A good resource to help identify how you are feeling can be found with a quick Google search for a "feelings wheel." Using a tool like this can help you narrow down your emotions from broad feelings such as "happy, sad, or fearful" to more precise ones like "hopeful, hurt, or helpless." This will help you discover how you are feeling at a deeper level. Take a moment to write down some emotions you identify. Revealing your emotions is an empowering step to help you honor them.

Release the emotions

Now that you have revealed your emotions, you can release them, which is a process that will require repeating. Releasing emotions isn't an easy, one-time event that eliminates all your worries, but it affects how your emotions affect *you*.

Releasing your emotions is a conscious effort that should be done as often as needed.

It isn't an easy process, and like me, you may be tempted to suppress them, but sharing how you feel is critical. We tend to attempt to control a situation by trying to over-control our emotions, but we must remember that bottling up our feelings is like that beach ball bound to rise to the surface.

In my experience, releasing my emotions to friends has been extremely helpful. We will talk more about that, but the primary person I encourage you to release them to is God. Who better to release the feelings in your heart than to the One who created it?

After revealing how you feel, releasing those feelings to God loosens the grip those emotions have on your heart. When we release the hold that fear, anxiety, loneliness, or grief may have on us, we create room for God to fill the space with His goodness, wisdom, and presence.

God wants to hear from you and help you with the roller-coaster of emotions. In 1 Peter 5:7 (NIV), He invites us to "Cast all your anxiety on him because he cares for you."

One way to do that is to write down the emotions you've revealed and one by one, imagine yourself, handing (or "casting") them to God. Actually visualize yourself "releasing" them to the Father. Will there be tears? Maybe. Will it be worth it? Absolutely.

You can also invite God into this process simply by speaking out loud to Him. You can be honest about your emotions and see how God meets you in that place. As you release your feelings to God, you can share with Him not only how you feel but explore why you feel this way.

Going to God, your trustworthy Father, with your feelings is the first step, but identifying a trusted friend or two is a great next step. Going to friends who can understand and uplift you in this season is a way to release your emotions and walk out the instruction found in Galatians 6:2 (NIV), "Carry each other's burdens, and in this way, you will fulfill the law of Christ."

Talking through how you feel with trusted friends can provide clarity and camaraderie, allowing you to be cared for by others. By talking with others about how you are feeling, you are not only honoring your emotions but releasing them and refusing to ignore them.

Another option to release your emotions is to journal. Grabbing a spiral notebook and pen can make a world of difference. Journaling is a great tool you can practice, helping you release and process your emotions. There is no wrong way to journal; just start! You can start by releasing one emotion at a time. Just use the pen in your hand to write what's on your heart and in your head.

The first several days and weeks as the mom of a high school student were tough for me.

Journaling in that season of my life proved to be very therapeutic and beneficial, as I was able to release my honest feelings about my son growing up and the shift I felt in motherhood.

This form of release can be helpful for anyone, but especially those who feel like you can't talk to God or don't have trusted friends available. You can find a few journaling prompts at the end of this chapter.

Reframe your thoughts.

Remember that revealing and releasing emotions is an event that will likely require repeating and intentionality, and the third step is no different. Reframing thoughts is something I began to do daily. It was like going from being a passenger on the rollercoaster to being the operator of it. Reframing wandering thoughts with solid truth from scripture changes everything.

During that time, the darkness consistently whispered defeating, fear-based, and negative thoughts. The only way to battle the thoughts that fueled my feelings was to reframe them. I had to reframe the words and worries that consumed me, and there were no other words to suffice other than the Word of God. This step allowed me to remind myself of what is true, to rely on God, and to recall His past faithfulness. I used the verse found in 2 Corinthians 10:5, took every thought captive, and made it obedient to Christ. As I was aware of the negative thoughts, I would stop immediately and recall a verse that spoke truth, pray, and ask God to help me see the situation as He does or recall His faithfulness in the past.

When your darkness whispers lies, combat it with the truth in God's Word. Challenge each thought fueling the rollercoaster by praying, finding a verse that speaks directly to your situation, listening to worship music, or reframing the thought through the lens of scripture.

A great way to reframe your thoughts is to return to the list of emotions you've revealed and find a verse that applies to that emotion or situation. Then, reframe it using scripture. An example of that is below:

Thought: What if my son/daughter starts hanging out with the wrong crowd?

Emotion: Fear

Scripture:
"Flee the evil desires of youth and pursue righteousness, faith, love, and peace, along with those who call on the Lord out of a pure heart." 2 Timothy 2:22, NIV

Reframe: I believe _____ will flee evil desires and choose friends who have a pure heart and pursue righteousness and peace.

The process of Revealing, Releasing, and Reframing is a practical way for you to feel empowered to embrace the highs, lows, and everything in between. The journey of motherhood in this season can be one of complicated emotions yet one of celebration. Your son/daughter is loved dearly, not only by you but by God. Trust Him not only with the rollercoaster of emotions you are feeling but with your son/daughter as well. Emotions themselves are not bad; God gave us emotions, and they point to a deeper need and longing that brings us to Him. In my journey through this season, I wouldn't have made it without prayer, so I consider it an extreme privilege to pray for you right now.

God, thank you for the mom reading this book. I pray that she feels safe, loved, known, and cared for by You. Remind her that although she is a mom who tends to the needs of others, she is best refreshed when she allows You to tend to the needs of her heart. Draw her close and remind her of Your truth when she battles lies from the enemy. I pray she seeks You and surrenders her fears, doubts, and anxious thoughts to You daily. Allow her to be brave enough to reveal how she feels, release her feelings to You, and be renewed as she reframes her thoughts with Yours. Thank you for her life, love, and legacy. In Jesus name, Amen.

Next Steps

Below are journal prompts to help you identify and release any emotions.

- What about this season makes me _____ (insert emotion)
- Am I nervous because I feel that I can't protect him/her?
- Is there something I am afraid of?
- Do I feel like I'm losing control?
- Is there any area where I'm feeling rejection, stress, or grief?
- What about this season am I looking forward to?
- What am I thankful for in this season of life?
- Are there other things going on in my life that are affecting how I view this season of motherhood?
- Do I feel as if I'm no longer needed?
- What about this feels scary, lonely, or challenging?
- Do I have any unmet expectations? If so, what are they, and how do they make me feel?
- Do I have any unspoken expectations? If yes, what are they?
- Do I tend to believe that my child's performance is a reflection of me and my parenting?
- Am I trying to provide my child with something he/she didn't ask for?
- Am I parenting out of fear?
- Am I actually afraid my child will make some of the mistakes I made in high school?
- The worst thing I could imagine happening to my child in this season is _____. If that happened, would that affect God's character?

✳

Chapter 7

Faithful Foundations: Building Spiritual Resilience for Parents and Children

By Bonnie Shue McDonald

"HEAR, O ISRAEL: THE LORD OUR GOD, THE LORD IS ONE. YOU SHALL LOVE THE LORD OUR GOD WITH ALL YOUR HEART AND WITH ALL YOUR SOUL AND WITH ALL YOUR MIGHT. AND THESE WORDS THAT I COMMAND YOU TODAY SHALL BE ON YOUR HEART. YOU SHALL TEACH THEM DILIGENTLY TO YOUR CHILDREN, AND SHALL TALK OF THEM WHEN YOU SIT IN YOUR HOUSE, AND WHEN YOU WALK BY THE WAY, AND WHEN YOU LIE DOWN, AND WHEN YOU RISE. YOU SHALL BIND THEM AS A SIGN ON YOUR HAND, AND THEY SHALL BE AS FRONTLETS BETWEEN YOUR EYES. YOU SHALL WRITE THEM ON THE DOORPOSTS OF YOUR HOUSE AND ON YOUR GATES."
DEUTERONOMY 6:4-9, ESV

Panic spread down the beach as the mom frantically looked through each gathering of families. "Have you seen a boy about this high?" She motioned about four feet. "Brown hair and in red swim trunks? He was right here and now we cannot find him. His name is Dylan."

Rapidly, the search spread, and we looked around to locate our own kids. "Okay, someone stay with the kids and the rest go look, now! No, wait. *Pray.* God, let this young man be found safe in Jesus' name. Amen." We were searching and praying. Up and down the beach, checking the water, spreading the word to other groups. We didn't even now know which ones were the boy's parents, but we were all combing the beach, the water, and the dunes. All the groups of bodies suddenly seemed to appear about four feet tall, with brown hair, and wearing red swim trunks. How could we tell them all apart?

"Lord, help him to be found."

Some families hadn't caught on to the problem yet, but we yelled to ask them to join the search. We moved so far from our own group that we decided to turn back and scour the other direction. "Lord, help us find this boy!" Hundreds were now searching for Dylan along the Carolina shore. We heard the crowd erupt about 200 yards from us. "Lord, let it be good news, please. Let him not be in the water." We couldn't bear to look, and the mass of people was so thick we couldn't see what was happening. The crowd moved toward the sand, away from the water, and cheers erupted. One of the dads in our group walked down the beach to gather the news.

"They found him! The young boy, Dylan, was found! Unhurt and safe." What a relief it was for everyone on the beach who was looking. We were sure his parents had just experienced many of the emotions of life in a twenty-minute time frame...along with the rest of us thinking about it as if it were our own child.

Did that sinking feeling grip you with nausea for the parents of the lost child on the beach? Me too! But we can look for the signs of God's power wherever we are at the moment. Communication in every aspect, prayer, and community was right there on that beach. It was amazing for this to occur among a group of strangers who only knew the one name needed to find this young man.

Shepherding our children as they make the transition to middle school can feel similar at times to the angst that arose in the panicked crowd. Overwhelming. Dreadful. Wearying. Lonely.

With these feelings and others you may experience, please know that you are not alone. Not only is God with you, but other moms feel exactly the same way. Your child is going through a transition and so are you! It is a stretching and molding to the shape the Potter is making. The hard things, the fiery trials, and the inevitable experiences will shape you for future opportunities. It might take 40 years for you to see the fruit in your child, or it may be 40 days. In this precious time, hang on to your Heavenly Father with all your heart.

Jesus is the One we know who walks with us in all transitions in life. Philippians 2:9 (ESV) says, "Therefore God exalted him to the highest place and gave him the name that is above every name, that at the name of Jesus, every knee should bow, in heaven and on earth and under the earth, and every tongue acknowledge that Jesus Christ is Lord, to the glory of God the Father."

This chapter isn't a list of do's and don'ts or a specific formula to follow, but encouragement for your loving relationship with the Lord and subsequently with your child(ren). We know from their toddlerhood that practices are caught more than taught. They learn to use a tissue for their drippy nose by watching us use a tissue. They learn to put the tissue in the trash by watching us do the same. This is a season to press into the Lord Jesus Christ, just as every other season is. Releasing our children to the Lord is one of the most challenging and growth-filled journeys we can endeavor. It can be the most joyful and produce much fruit to be celebrated at every victory, although it might be a few years before you see the fruit that lasts. So grab your journal, pen, or highlighter and note what God reveals to you right here in the book while we walk this way together.

Help your children to see God at work in your own life and the lives of others. This happens through a genuine love relationship with our Heavenly Father.

Cling to His word, and He will guide you. Talk about it when you get up and lay down and walk in His ways. Pray with them and for them. If your relationship isn't where you want it to be, pray. Joel 2:13 says, "Return to the Lord your God, for he is gracious and merciful, slow to anger and abounding in steadfast love."

Growing up in a liturgical church, we sang this every Sunday. At the time, I had no idea that it was scripture. Now I am grateful that I have it permanently etched in the songs of my heart, but I wish someone would have told me we were singing scripture.

Think about your practices at church and around the

house. Do your kids know why you do the things you do? Do you talk about the scriptures and read them together? Don't let defeat set in here if you do not currently have the habits you would like. You can start them right now, right where you are.

Pick one habit for yourself and let your children learn with you in age-appropriate ways. The oldest will "get it" the most. The littles will glean what they may according to their unique design. Maybe the first habit is prayer and teaching them a simple prayer-time format of praise, confession, thanksgiving, and requests. Guide them aloud by praising the Father for His attributes. Relieve yourself of the burden of what to pray, and choose a resource to help you, like Moms In Prayer (MIP).

Here it is, years later, and I am still using the MIP attributes list to praise our Father for a different attribute each month. This month, the attribute is goodness. So, I use a scripture referring to God's goodness. For confession, choose a verse related to confession, and do the same for thanksgiving. Prayer requests come at the very end. If this is a new habit, make the prayer time as short or as long as is suitable for your family. It can take place on your daily commute, around the dinner table, on the way to or from evening activities, or at home in the evening. Continue to meditate on Deuteronomy 6:4-9: "When I walk by the way, when I lie down and when I rise." Your solo prayer time can happen during household chores or even in the shower.

Here is a sample prayer to help guide you and your kids:

Praise:
Lord, I praise you for your goodness.

You are good and upright. (Psalm 25:8)
I give thanks to you for you are good and your mercy endures forever. (1 Chronicles 16:34)
Help me to love you more God.

Confession:

God, forgive me for the things I have done wrong. I repent, then, and turn to you, so that my sins may be wiped out, and that times of refreshing may come from you. (Acts 3:19)

Help me to not repeat the same mistakes. Help me to learn. It is your goodness that leads me to repentance. (Romans 2:4)

Thanksgiving:

You tell us in Colossians 4:2 to devote ourselves to prayer, being watchful and thankful. Thank you, God, for this time to pray. Thank you for the freedom to pray freely at any time. Thank you for helping us learn to pray more often.

Petitions / Requests:

Personalize your prayer requests here.

When praying in this manner, there is a path to follow. You can pick out the verses to use at the beginning of a month and use them throughout the month. Familiarity with the verses and the attribute will cause you and your children to look for God's goodness. This provides an opportunity for discussion and answering questions as they arise. Make it as formal or informal as your family prefers. "Hey, God. Can I talk to you now?" is a great way to build a prayer time. Resist making it rule-oriented or having a right or wrong way. If the prayer veers off the path, it's okay to go in that direction and then get back on the path. Many great methods can be explored. Even for adults, a pattern like this does not get old or boring but opens us to the possibility of praying different scriptures each month of the year.

Many people do not pray often because they do not have a path. Or they have a memorized prayer that stays the same all the time. Help your child develop a lifetime habit of prayer by following a path. Sitting down together to choose verses is a great way to share an experience and allow open discussion to see what verses they might like to use. Don't hesitate to ask Google, "What verses include confession?" Just help your children confirm that the source is valid.

Be intentional about having your own "quiet time" when your children can observe you. (Even though their sleep time is the most likely time to get time alone with God). Susanna Wesley, mother of theologian John Wesley, and hymn writer Charles Wesley, had a total of 19 children. She covered her head with a "prayer apron" and taught her kids not to disturb her time alone with the Lord[9]. Try following her example in a way that makes sense at your home (probably not with a prayer apron over your head), and let your children see your habits so they can learn from you. Everyone in the whole family will grow in the process.

Prayer doesn't have to be the first habit you develop. Others are Bible reading and journaling about the reading. These three habits can be caught as well as taught. A simple Bible reading plan and daily SOAP (a journaling acrostic) are

---

[9] Wesley, Susanna. *Susanna Wesley: The Complete Writings*. Edited by Charles Wallace, Zondervan, 1985.

just two of many ways to journal. (See resources at the end of the chapter)

Daily SOAP is simple for many. A former student in our youth group shared this method with fellow students in her 8th-grade year. That was 15 years ago, and I still use this method, as it allows me to process the verses in a simple yet memorable manner.

S- Scripture. After reading a passage of scripture, choose the verse or verses that grab your attention. Or perhaps verses you do not understand. Write those verses out in your journal beside the letter S.

O- Observation. Write down what you observe in the passage by the letter O. Who is speaking? To whom are they speaking? What is the subject? Why is this happening? When is it happening? What is the setting? Are there words you don't know? Look them up and write the definitions.

A- Application. How does God intend for this scripture to be used? Is there a truth to be known? A promise or conviction? What principle can you practice? Write these in the journal by the letter A. No special journal is needed. Choosing your own is part of making a SOAP journal special.

P- Prayer. Write your prayer to God by the letter P in response to what you have learned in today's SOAP.

Recently, I went down memory lane, looking through my journals back to 2013. There are areas of growth in trust and obedience. There are thoughts where I wondered, "Who wrote this?" I also use my journal to record gratitudes daily, following the example of Ann Voskamp,[10] and number them successively. In reviewing my old journal, I recalled the places where God helped me to have a better perspective because of a scripture reading or teaching I listened to that particular day. I can easily identify many places where God was at work then and celebrate the small steps of progress since I know some of the outcomes now.

These practices help your children learn to notice where God is at work. Intentionally make connections between what is happening in life and what has been prayed. Develop a dinner-time discussion that includes where they have observed God at work in their day, maybe in the beautiful sunrise or a rain shower that was badly needed. A friend could be in a hard situation, and we lift them in prayer together so that they might see a glimmer of hope. Or someone might have overslept and made it to school on time anyway. As we examine the day together and look for areas that we have prayed for together, we can see what He is doing that is meaningful and serves a purpose in our lives. This helps us to identify that he is at work and wants us to join him. Our God is personal. He orchestrates what is happening right in our daily lives.

Foster community support for your children and yourself. The life of Paul can help us see that a mentor like Paul is invaluable. Who is "a Paul" in your life as a parent? Are there people in your family, neighborhood, or church who share your values, faith in Christ, and parenting experiences? Do you have friends who are educators in the middle grades and

[10] Voskamp, Ann. *One Thousand Gifts: A Dare to Live Fully Right Where You Are*. Zondervan, 2011.

would have a parent's perspective? There are cultural differences from region to region, and what may be a challenge at one middle school may not be an issue in another area. Having a parent mentor in your area who can help guide you on the local challenges will be helpful. Some areas may have gang-related problems. For other areas, it may be drug-related or vaping. Being involved with parents in your local area who have experienced the current issues will prove valuable to you and your child. Pray for God to help you find someone who can be a mentor in parenting and life.

Talk to your children. This includes the pitfalls. Be honest and open about obstacles they might face so they will recognize them. Help them plan their response. In our home, we had a phrase they could text me or if we were talking on the phone. I knew what the phrase meant. Our phrase: "Would you put my jeans in the dryer?". This meant, "Wherever I am and whatever I am doing, I need you to come and get me now." We promised to always pick them up, take them home, and discuss when they were ready. This small act reassures them of a way out of whatever situation occurs and keeps dialogue open.

Maybe a different mindset exists, and you may not yet recognize it in parenting. A little pride that says, "Not my child. They don't even know any of the things that older kids do with phones or texting, and they only use their phones to text me to pick them up after practice." Parents who have experienced their children getting in "phone trouble" often DO NOT want to talk about it because they are embarrassed that their child did it. They want to forget that it happened.

A wise educator of two now-grown adults shared that

the parents who think their children will not do anything wrong are often the ones who are blindsided by a big blowup at school. Don't let this be you because of a lack of communication. Do not let shame caused by Satan keep you from talking with your children to help them avoid the pitfalls facing them today. Can it be embarrassing? Yes! As parents, do we consider that we have "taught them better?" Yes, we are trying our best. We have taught them, but they are still going to do wrong things and make wrong choices. We can know we have done everything possible if we have made them aware of potential happenings with cell phones and pics and the consequences that follow.

Be transparent. Help them by checking their phones regularly. Be real and be in prayer. A discussion like this is a great time to pray *with* your child. Phones are not the only area of concern, but you will need other adults to help you in the areas that may fall into your blind spot.

Nurturing community among like-minded students helps when there are one or two in the group whose families have similar values or perhaps are involved at the same church. There may be groups at school, community groups, church groups such as FCA, youth groups, and extracurricular interests with adult leaders you trust. Help your children to have the courage to try out a few different ones until they find a good fit. Having a friend in on it from the beginning provides an ally, especially if parents have children near the same age and can go together. Adjust your own life to build in the freedom to make this possible for your children. We have only a few years to make an eternal difference in their lives, so seize the time now.

Conclusion

When the beach ordeal was over and Dylan, the lost boy on the beach was found, there was a celebration! What could have been a nightmare for a lifetime was only terrifying for a short while of 20ish minutes. As you navigate this transitional season of the middle school years, be encouraged that it will present challenges you have not faced before. The steps you choose to take because of your obedience to our Father will prepare you and your child for the unknown. When the unthinkable happens, you will know you have done your part. Trust God's word in Proverbs 22:6, "Train up a child in the way he should go and when he is old, he will not depart from it."

We can't shield our children from the hurts of this world, but we can help them know the One who will carry us through those adversities. When adversities come as they will, connecting with God through prayer will help their faith in Him grow. Ours too! Reading and journaling the Bible, praying the scriptures, and talking about it helps develop a love relationship with God. Soon, we realize that this time has helped prepare us for the next one and the next one.

Lord, we praise you for being our sovereign God and in control of every single aspect of our lives and the lives of our children. Forgive us when we make mistakes intentionally or unintentionally. Help us to be more pleasing to you. Thank you for your transforming power. Thank you for these children who bless our lives. Thank you for the community you are preparing for us and the friends and family that will help us through this season. Help us to be the parents you have designed us to be — the ones you have chosen to train up this child(ren), to read and pray your word and become more obedient and faithful with each passing day. Continually help our ears hear a word behind us saying, "This is the way, walk in it" when you turn to the right and when you turn to the left. (Isaiah 30:21) Help us to trust you with each and every day. In Jesus' name, we pray. Amen.

Next Steps

Seven Things to Pray for Your Children from DesiringGod.org

1. That Jesus will call them and no one will hinder them from coming. Matthew 19:13-15

2. That they will respond in faith to Jesus' faithful, persistent call. 2 Peter 3:9

3. That they will experience sanctification through the transforming work of the Holy Spirit and will increasingly desire to fulfill the greatest commandments. Matthew 22:37-29

4. That they will not be unequally yoked in intimate relationships, especially marriage. 2 Corinthians 6:14

5. That their thoughts will be pure. Philippians 4:8

6. That their hearts will be stirred to give generously to the Lord's work. Exodus 35:29

7. That when the time is right, they will GO! Matthew 28:18-20

Additional Resources

7 Things to Pray for My Children Printable[11]

Prayer Journal - Valmariepaper.com[12]

Power of a Praying Parent Book of Prayers - Stormie Omartian[13]

Power of a Praying Parent Perpetual Calendar - Stormie Omartian[14]

American Bible Society Daily Bible Reading[15]

Experiencing God Day by Day Podcast by Dr. Richard Blackaby[16]

---

[11] Piper, David. "Seven Things to Pray for Your Children." Desiring God, 18 June 2019, www.desiringgod.org/articles/seven-things-to-pray-for-your-children. Accessed 1 Aug. 2024.

[12] ValMarie Paper. Prayer Journal. ValMarie Paper, www.valmariepaper.com. Accessed 1 Aug. 2024.

[13] Omartian, Stormie. Power of a Praying Parent Book of Prayers. Harvest House Publishers, 1995.

[14] Omartian, Stormie. Power of a Praying Parent Perpetual Calendar. Harvest House Publishers, 2000.

[15] American Bible Society. "Daily Bible Reading." American Bible Society, www.americanbible.org/resources/daily-bible-reading/. Accessed 1 Aug. 2024.

[16] Blackaby, Richard. Experiencing God Day by Day Podcast. Blackaby Ministries International, https://experiencinggoddaybydaypodcast.libsyn.com/. Accessed 1 Aug. 2024.

Chapter 8

---✳---

Teaching Through Transitions: Balancing Classroom and Home Life

By Takhia Gaither

Ahhh, teaching ... The profession from which all others flow. It's great, rewarding, endearing, demanding, and some days downright unnerving, yet we keep returning to it. But then you hit that major crossroads of parenthood and teacherhood. More specifically, for me, motherhood and teacherhood. When your children are not school-aged, it seems a lot easier to manage the mom guilt of going back to work to care for someone else's child for 6 – 7 hours a day. Just when you think you're okay, your child starts school, and you see first-day pics as you scroll through social media. You realize that you may not get those opportunities to take pictures because you're the teacher: you have to show up on the first day too! Welcome to my world! At least, it was up until the pandemic happened.

When my oldest son started school, I saw all of his first days via the pictures I hoped someone else remembered to take. One year, I specifically remember getting his first day of school picture at the end of the day when I picked him up because his father didn't think about taking them that morning. It was kind of devastating, especially since I was starting a new teaching assignment at a new school the same day! There was this all-day internal battle of, "But I couldn't see him off to school. I guess this is just my life from here on out."

Then came the "fun" of 2020. I don't say that to be insensitive to the many things that took place during that time and the lives lost, but I can honestly say I learned a lot about myself and the profession I'd been committed to for double-digit years. The way society upheld and discarded teachers was so jarring. One day, we were the heroes for persisting through the ups, downs, and uncertainties and continuing to teach. Then, we became the villains who weren't doing enough. It was so bi-polar. However, that time gave me the "break" I needed.

Virtual teaching made me sick. Literally. I was diagnosed with an autoimmune condition in 2009 and until 2020 had done well managing the symptoms and flare-ups. It didn't take long during the remainder of the 2019-2020 school year for me to know that trying to maintain that level and amount of speaking while staring at a screen for the upcoming school year was not going to happen. I attempted to go on medical leave at the start of the school year, but teacher guilt gripped me hard. I taught an AP, (Advanced Placement) course. The students had to get ready for the exam the following May and it would be unfair to leave them with nothing. Despite my concerns, I started the school year with my son in one room, myself in another, and my then toddler seated right next to me all day as I taught. Many outside of education didn't realize the expectation of teachers during that time was to basically ignore the needs of your children who were home with you and focus solely on those in your cyber classroom.

During a normal school year, when I am in the building designated for me to teach and my children are in the care of another trusted adult, I can understand that expectation. Being in my home watching my own child struggle was not something that I was going to be able to do. I officially left the classroom in November 2020 at Thanksgiving break. Having the weight of teaching lifted from my shoulders allowed me to focus on my children, their education, and their needs. Although there were other struggles of life happening at the time, having the time to focus solely and primarily on them during the school day was invaluable.

The following year, I extended my leave and didn't return. I was excited to see my sons off to their first days of school! When my oldest left, I cried for a little bit because it dawned on me that I'd never been able to see him off. A few weeks later, when the younger one started pre-K, I was there to see him off as well. I could go on field trips and pop up for important days at school without having to check in and take a day off or leave sub plans. I could just decide to go, and it was such a wonderful feeling. I'd started my own business, and things were going well. One day, while working on something for a client, I decided to look up online teaching jobs for community colleges and tutoring opportunities. I'd always checked every once in a while just to see what was available in case I felt up to it. I kept the searches brief, and at the first sight of anything that felt like anxiety, I abandoned the search and continued to be content with being home.

Before going on leave, I prayed for direction. I needed to hear the Lord clearly on what to do. He said to go on leave, and I went. The end. In July of 2023, He started calling me back to the classroom. Like many of us do when we hear things from God that we don't want to hear, I tried to act like He didn't say that. I was hearing wrong and just being antsy because things were slowing down in business, and teaching was always a guaranteed check. As much as I tried to ignore it, it wouldn't go away. My parents brought up returning to the classroom during a random conversation, and my response was still "Meh." The last confirmation was hearing my Pastor say, "You have to go back. He's sending you back. Stop running." I cried like a baby for multiple reasons. One, because I'd heard God clearly, and that's always a reason for joy. But the flip side was that I was signing up to miss my children's days again, and I didn't want to do that. So, I was left with a decision. Should I answer the call or keep going with my own plans? Well, Proverbs 3:5-6 cleared that up immediately. "Trust in the Lord with all your heart; do not depend on your own understanding. Seek His will in all you do, and He will show you which path to take" (NLT).

Three weeks before school started, I went to the last job fair before the school year started. To notify applicants and interviewers of which entrance to use, there was a balloon display on the walkway leading to the door. As I prayed before going in, I remember saying out loud jokingly, "Hey God, those balloons are blue and white. Is that what I should look for?" I gathered my belongings, went inside, and wouldn't you know it, the colors of the school where I work are actually blue and white?! They had a math teacher transfer schools about an hour before the job fair started. The position was so newly vacated that it hadn't even been posted to the public pool. I walked out with a position and came home to tell my children I'd be returning to work. They were excited, but of course, there were questions. Would I be able to attend field trips? Could I still come on specific days? Would I be there in the morning to take them to school? As excited as I was to be returning to the classroom, I also felt despair. I felt like I was once again giving up my time to take care of everyone else's children.

The 2023-2024 school year was the trifecta of transitions for my children and me. My youngest was starting kindergarten, the oldest was starting middle school, and I was returning to the classroom. The thing about transitions is that they're really trial and error. Part of my ability to be able to transition well was coming to grips with the fact that sometimes, there are no answers. You just have to move along. Take each day as it comes. The Lord's prayer says, "Give us this day, our daily bread" (Matthew 6:11). When I was younger, I used to think that it referred to food. Now that I'm older and have studied more, I realize that bread is a metaphor. Jesus is the bread of life, so really, the prayer says, "Give me my dose of Jesus to get through today." I don't know about you, but I've had days where I felt like I needed extra doses. You have to breathe through it. Children are resilient. They have far more bounceback than we could ever imagine as parents. They will follow your lead. If you're in panic and disarray, they will be as well.

Maybe you're not returning to the classroom but are considering returning to work, changing shifts, or altering your day-to-day schedule while balancing the educational transitions of your children. This is for you. One thing is constant: Your children will always progress through school. That's what we raise them to do. What they will remember most is how you made time for them despite your schedule. They may not realize it up front but once they enter adulthood, they will. Trust me on that one! My bonus daughter just graduated college, and we had the most amazing "Thank you, Mom" talk. It made it all worth it!

As a mathematician and computer scientist, my world is filled with numbers and things that should happen in logical and sequential order. Although I have numbered the list below, I do not feel "married" to the order. Realistically, these can be one day at a time or all at the same time. (Have you really mothered if you haven't had to do everything all at the same time?) Don't let the numbers overwhelm you. Just go with the flow.

Next Steps:
1. **Stay as positive as possible.** I know this comes across as a "duh" suggestion, but hear me out. When we face adversities, it is natural and somewhat easier to pick out all the unfavorable things about it. Initially, we may need to run through the list of things to get them out of our systems and help the smoke clear. With as much apprehension as I had about returning to work, I made sure to reinforce the benefits of my doing so. I also highlighted the fact that we'd all be out of the house at the same time and off together

for most school vacation days. We tend to focus on the loss and absence of time instead of thinking about how to maximize the time we will have.

2. **Plan activities ahead of time.** When the school year started, I told my children I would try to attend one field trip for each of them and would attend all the important after-school events such as concerts, art shows, and conferences. I made sure they understood that I would show up as much as possible. I work relatively close to their schools, so for in-school events, I could pop in if I was free during my planning block. If you don't have that flexibility, keep a family calendar in a central location so everyone knows what and when the special school days and events are. That will help you plan accordingly.

3. **Take care of your home first.** Yes, it's a no-brainer, and it could have easily been #1, but it's still necessary to say. One of the things I realized when going out on medical leave was that the school was not concerned about my health and well-being. However, my children and family were. Before I decided to go on leave, I was experiencing a flare-up and decided to take a few days to get better. I sent in paperwork for a substitute, secured one, and even had a conversation with her about what my class would be doing and the support they may need. I emailed the appropriate persons and proceeded to rest. I ended up checking my work email because I was looking for a specific piece of information and received what I felt was an inappropriate email from a parent and an even more

inappropriate one from the principal regarding being out. From that day forward, I was free of teacher guilt. If I cease to exist, while multiple people will be affected, my children will suffer the most. No job is worth that.

4. **Check in with you often.** In the hustle and bustle of all the things, we sometimes avoid or ignore how or what we're feeling. We feel like we should just keep going, and at some point, we'll take care of whatever we need. But here's the thing, "some point" rarely, if ever comes, and before we know it we're overwhelmed, burnt out, and exhausted. At one time, I was a workaholic. It was the way I chose to fight depression. It didn't work well and came crashing down. Pay attention to the signs your body gives you to rest, slow down, or just stop and, as they say in many churches with the announcements, "govern yourself accordingly."

5. **Leave work at work.** When you're a teacher, this one seems almost impossible, but it was really a game changer for me. I used to bring home tons of papers to grade and stacks of books to write lesson plans. I'd spend all evening working on those things with just a break for dinner, barely spending time with my children. When virtual learning became the mandate, I decided for my own sanity that after 4:00 pm, I would not do anything teacher-related. Going back into the classroom this year, I rarely brought work home. Sometimes, it was inevitable, but most days, I only transported my laptop back and forth because I didn't want it to stay in my classroom. Not having

to be "Takhia the Teacher" after school hours allowed me to be Mom, Entrepreneur, Minister, or just be me!

Most of these tips are things you probably already know, think about, or do. However, when all the things come quickly, the overwhelm and guilt set in, and you're trying to balance everything, they are often pushed to the side and overlooked because they're simplistic. I am by no means an expert. As I said in the beginning, the way to go through things is to understand that there is not one right answer. The answer is the one that works for you. Maybe you're good at time management or have children who are asleep by early evening, so bringing work home isn't a bother to you. That's great! Go with what you know. The point of these simple steps is to make you slow down and think about what you are doing or not doing and make changes to help the transitions go smoother. Nothing will be perfect, but there are ways to make it seem very close to it!

Chapter 9

———✳———

Learning to Let Go When the Road Looks Different: A Mother's Guide to Trusting God with Her Child's Future

By Amy E. Oyster

"WHAT I'M LEARNING IS THAT THE GOOD NEWS OF OUR FAITH ISN'T FOUND IN AVOIDING THE PAIN, BUT IN LIVING THROUGH THE LOSS, WALKING THROUGH THE ASHES, AND STACKING THE LOGS ONCE MORE KNOWING THEY COULD BURN DOWN AGAIN. WHAT HAS BEEN GROWING INSIDE OF ME IS A CONFIDENCE THAT WHATEVER IT IS WE PUT OUR EFFORTS INTO, IT'S GOD'S, AND HE CAN DO WHATEVER HE WANTS WITH WHAT WE BUILD IN OUR LIVES." MARIA GOFF, *LOVE LIVES HERE*[17]

At 3:30 in the morning, something woke me up and told me to check on him. He was 17 months old, but I'd put him to bed with a fever. When I walked in, I wasn't prepared for what I saw. His arms were straight up

---

[17] Goff, Maria. *Love Lives Here: Finding What You Need in a World Telling You What You Want.* B&H Publishing Group, 2017.

in the air, fists clenched, and eyes rolled back in his head. I honestly didn't know what was happening, but I thought he was dying. I rushed to pick him up and assure him mommy was there and he was okay, but his muscles were so stiff and firm that I had to lay him down. Within seconds, his body began to shake and jerk violently. Frightened, scared, and pregnant with baby number two, I begged God, "Please don't take my child." Once the convulsions subsided, he began to cry. Only then could I try to console him. His body was on fire! Over the next twelve months, Sam suffered nine more grand mal seizures. We were told they were febrile in nature, but they became so prevalent he was put on a daily preventative and later diagnosed with epilepsy.

I was so engrossed in managing the seizures and taking care of his baby sister that I declined the parent-teacher conference that was offered at the end of his preschool year. He was two, for heaven's sake, and honestly, it seemed like he was passing with flying colors. He'd entered that year knowing all his numbers, letters, colors, and shapes. He was fascinated with learning, an absolute sponge for information, and had an impeccable memory. Just shy of three years old, he was already reading Dr. Seuss books to his little sister. But his teacher stopped me in the carline and said, "I need to talk to you; I have some concerns." What in the world? What possible concerns could have developed between November and May? He was doing fantastic! What I learned was that while academically he was shining, socially, he lagged. Developmental delays were beginning to surface, and a battery of tests later revealed signs of Level 1 Autism, or Asperger's Syndrome.

Sam was diagnosed with Asperger's when he was four years old, the same time his neurologist confirmed his having epilepsy. He was my first child, so as a new mom, I watched and paid close attention to all the pertinent milestones. I tried not to worry when other children were meeting them, and he was not. The pediatrician even said not to worry, "He was on the late side of normal." But at two years old, deep down, I knew something was different. The tantrums were extreme; he was fixated on certain toys or objects, and his communication, while remarkable in some ways, did not match his peers. My heart sank! I could not understand what was happening, what this meant long term, or even what we were dealing with for the immediate future. As an educator, I knew he would need assistance and likely accommodations in the classroom. He had been receiving speech services through the public school system since he was three, but his new Autism diagnosis gave him eligibility for a full IEP (Individual Education Plan). In addition to speech and occupational therapies, Sam would need increased structure and strategies to help him focus and transition smoothly to various activities within a given school day. I was afraid of what would be required for my child to succeed. I was afraid that it would be too much. I was afraid no one would be there to step in to protect him when other children were unkind.

I just wanted him to have a "normal" life. I wanted him to be okay. I wanted him to make it. I'd wanted that for as long as I could remember– since the seizures began, since I'd watched the cashier at one of my favorite local stores ignore him as he smiled excitedly and waved and said, "Hi! Hi Mister! Hi!." Since I'd learned he had Asperger's–All I ever wanted was for him to be okay. But I found myself consumed with fear. I was afraid this big, nasty world would swallow him whole because he was genuinely kind, tender, sensitive, curious, and naive to the social nuances of the broken world around him. I knew one day someone would deliberately hurt his feelings, and he wouldn't understand why. I could no longer protect him, and I couldn't stand it! Then the day came...it was time to leave what felt like the safety and security net of elementary school and transition to the big, unknown, unkind world of middle school. Sam was going to middle school, and I was a nervous wreck. How in the world would we make it?

We had been fortunate enough in elementary to have been surrounded by a team of teachers, therapists, and counselors who knew Sam, loved him, and were *for* him. To move out from under that hedge of protection, that shelter, was a big deal for any child, much less a child who needed an extra measure of guidance and care. But somewhere along the way, I realized Sam wasn't the one who was anxious or uneasy; it was me! Sam was ready. He had been adequately prepared. He had been recommended for Accelerated Math and was excited to meet his new math teacher. He'd even considered trying band since you couldn't try out for sports teams until the 7th grade. So what was my problem? I'd gone right back to fearing the worst, just as I did when I walked into his nursery at 3:30 am. I feared what I couldn't see–the unknown. Whereas elementary school represented safety, security, love and protection, and loads of parental involvement, middle school represented the struggle for independence, the desire to fit in, an abundance of hormones and drama, insecurities galore, and very little parental involvement. I wasn't ready for Sam to face all of that. I wasn't sure

Sam was ready, but it was time for him to go. I could not hold him back. Moving to middle school would require a whole new level of trust and letting go.

Dear friend, I know exactly what you're going through as you enter this new season. I know that fear and worry and angst that tugs at your heart and plagues your mind. The one that continues to drip the "what if" statements and play out all the potential scenarios. You cannot live there. It will consume you and stunt your child's growth. It will rob your joy and chip away at your child's confidence. If they are to grow and become everything they are meant to be, we must get out of the way! We must fully embrace and celebrate the person God has created them to be. God made them special and unique in their own way. What a beautiful gift! While certain tasks may require a little extra effort or may be more challenging to them than others, those differences are not without purpose and intention. He makes no mistakes. The psalmist says, "For you created my inmost being; you knit me together in my mother's womb. I praise you because I am fearfully and wonderfully made; your works are wonderful, I know that full well" (Psalm 139:13-14,NIV).

As a mom of a child with Asperger's, I had to come to grips with the reality that his road would likely look different than mine or even what I'd envisioned for him, and that was okay. I realized that I had my own set of experiences and expectations, subconscious as they were, that I was drawing from, and until I released those wholeheartedly, I was not free to be the parent Sam needed me to be. I may not have been able to keep him from stumbling, but I could surely help him get back up, brush him off, and send him on his way. My job was not to remove the roadblocks but to help him as he encountered them.

I knew there would be some tough times–and there were. Middle school is hard for everyone. There were celebratory moments and moments of great distress. There was deep joy and satisfaction in learning a new instrument and acing a math class two grade levels ahead of his own, and there were social situations that didn't make sense to him, misunderstandings that left him hurt, confused, and even angry. There were kids who said some very unkind things that left him questioning, doubting, and unsure of himself. While it's these very circumstances that will break a mother's heart, we are giving our child one of the greatest gifts when we choose to allow them to walk through these valleys *without* stepping in, letting them figure it out, knowing all the while we will be there waiting on the other side. We cannot prevent the pain from happening, but we can equip them with how to handle adversity. Our job is to continue to cheer them on from the sidelines, helping them learn to navigate these hardships successfully while granting them space to grow and shine, becoming stronger as they do along the way because they *can* do it! And they *will* be okay!

If you're familiar with the Bible, it's compelling that scripture often references God's people as sheep because we really are a stubborn lot! I finally realized when there was nothing tangible I could do, I could pray. And that, sweet friend, is the most powerful and effective thing to do anyway. I began to pray three very specific prayers for Sam--to make one good friend, to have one teacher he connected with and who was for him, and to find one activity he enjoyed participating in. He didn't need a multitude of friends and activities. He didn't need to be Mr. Popular, Mr. Athletic, or head of this and that. He needed to be Sam. And I wanted him to be the best Sam he could be. If he had those three things, his transition to middle school would be an absolute WIN!

Lastly, I had to stay in the game. And you do, too! You are, and always will be, your child's biggest cheerleader. In the Kentucky Derby, it's commonplace for trainers to put blinders or blinkers on their racehorses to keep them focused on what's in front of them, limiting the surrounding distractions. We have to do the same. We cannot become distracted or encumbered by who's doing what around us. The comparison game never works. When we stay singularly focused on what is in front of us, we can celebrate, support, and advocate for our children and be the parents they need us to be.

I can't say the road will be entirely easy. Jesus never promised us that. But I will tell you that as a mom, watching her child grow and develop into the person he is meant to be is one of the greatest blessings and the most beautiful gifts in the world. God did provide all I asked that 6th grade year: one friend, one teacher, and one activity. But even if he didn't, I had to trust that his plan was better. He was working out his purpose in both Sam's life and mine "for our good and his glory" (Romans 8:28). I am so proud of who Sam is. He will enter his sophomore year of high school this coming school year and has grown into an incredible young man. Stay the course, mama! You can do it, and so can your precious child.

So what about you? What is it that you're struggling or

wrestling with? Where do you need to let go and trust God with his plan instead of your own? I've listed some journaling or reflection questions below and encourage you to answer these for yourself. After you've done that, I encourage you to get with a trusted friend or family member to share your responses. Choose someone with whom you can be honest and vulnerable and who will hold space for you and your heart.

Journal/Reflection Questions:

1. What is it specifically that you're fearful or afraid of? Why?

2. Where do you need to let go and trust God to take care of your child?

3. What three things (specific) can you be praying for your child as they enter their middle school years?

Chapter 10

---*---

Embracing the Journey: Encouragement + Hope for Homeschooling Moms

By Chelsea Garofalo

"AND LET US NOT GROW WEARY OF DOING GOOD, FOR IN DUE SEASON WE WILL REAP, IF WE DO NOT GIVE UP."
GALATIANS 6:9, ESV

I never planned on being a homeschool mom. Even though I was homeschooled at different times during my childhood, I never envisioned homeschooling my own children.

If there's one thing I have learned over the last couple of years, it's that homeschooling is not just an educational choice; it is a commitment, a labor of love, and a lifestyle.

I went to college to become an elementary teacher and always thought my kids would one day attend the same school where I taught. Homeschooling my children was never part of my plan, but as Woody Allen famously said, "If you want to make God laugh, tell him about your plans."

Whether you're exploring the world of homeschooling, you're just starting out, or you've been at it for over a decade, my goal for this chapter is for you to finish reading with a sense of hope, inspiration, motivation, and encouragement-or simply the confidence to begin this journey with certainty.

This verse at the beginning of this chapter from Galatians speaks directly to my heart as a home educator because it echoes both the beauty and the challenges of this unique journey. *Weary. Give up.* I've felt both as a homeschooling mom. *Doing good. Reap.* I'm starting to see and feel the fruit resulting from this work. There are many days when I am just so weary and feel completely burned out. And then there are the days when I see glimmers of the harvest on its way. Galatians 6:9 serves as a daily reminder for my husband and me that the hard work of homeschooling will reap a harvest. That even on the days when I feel *tired* or like giving up on the idea of home education, it's still *worth it.*

Friend, if God has called you to this adventure and you don't lose heart, I truly believe your efforts will bear fruit in your children's lives.

I taught for several years in the classroom before I "retired." When my oldest daughter was younger, I spent some time teaching online part-time, and it was during this period that I began seriously considering where she would go to school one day. As I started exploring the various public and private schools in our area, I discovered hybrid homeschooling and was immediately drawn to the model. I strongly desired to be actively involved in my daughter's education and still retain some of the traditional school experiences I wanted my children to have.

Fast forward, and we now have two girls starting kindergarten and third grade. We are entering our fifth year of hybrid homeschooling. Our daughters attend a private school two days a week and are at home the other days, completing their lessons, school work, and other various activities we do together. When other moms or friends ask me if I recommend this homeschooling model, my response is always, "This is what's currently working for our family and what my husband and I feel called to do. We genuinely approach the decision one year at a time."

Public school, private school, full-time homeschool, hybrid homeschool, online school... There are so many ways to educate our children, but which way is the right way?

Over the years, I've had many conversations with friends and family discussing the benefits and challenges of various educational options. Recognizing the privilege of having a choice, there are days when I wonder if we are making the right decision. In my heart, I truly believe that the most important step we can take is to seek wisdom from the Lord through prayer, trusting that He will guide us to what's best for our family. This year, we are starting our fifth year of the hybrid model, but we don't know if we will continue on this course for middle or high school. I told my friend the other day that if she chooses to homeschool one year, it doesn't mean she has to do it the next. If you're deciding to homeschool your child for Kindergarten, it doesn't mean you're committing to the process for the next 13 years. It's important and helpful to approach it as a year-by-year decision guided by prayer.

At the beginning of our homeschool journey, I found myself second-guessing my abilities and feeling inadequate, but I reminded myself that homeschooling is considered one of the earliest forms of education. In many cultures throughout history, children were primarily educated at home by their parents or community members before formal schools became widespread. Home-centered education has been the norm in numerous societies throughout history. The earliest method of education was informal and home-based, usually occurring within the family and community. Parents, elders, and community members were responsible for imparting essential knowledge and skills to children. This included practical life skills such as hunting, farming, cooking, and crafting, as well as moral, cultural, and religious teachings.

Storytelling, apprenticeships, and hands-on learning were common methods used to educate the younger generation. Knowledge was passed down orally through stories, songs, and demonstrations. This informal approach to education was deeply integrated into daily life and varied greatly across different cultures and societies.

Today, there are several methods or approaches to homeschooling, each with its own philosophy and methodology. Some of the most common methods are Classical, Traditional, Montessori, Charlotte Mason, Unit Studies, and Online/Virtual Schooling. These methods provide flexibility and allow families to choose an approach that aligns with their educational philosophy, their child's learning style, and their specific educational goals. Many homeschooling families choose to blend elements from multiple methods to create a customized educational experience for their children. This chapter isn't about all the various homeschooling methods. However, if you are interested in learning more, or all of these choices sound overwhelming, there are excellent resources online, books, and podcast episodes that help explain each method and break them down.

People might assume I'm a great homeschool mom because of my background as a teacher, but I find that notion... amusing. My classroom teaching experience doesn't automatically translate into being great at homeschooling my own daughters. In fact, I have to work *really* hard to avoid letting my teaching style and experience from my years in the classroom influence how I educate my girls at home, where we eat, play, sleep, and do everything else together. In some ways, I feel like I am "retraining my brain" in what school can look and feel like. On homeschool days with my girls, I try to adapt to the mindset that the world is our classroom. Yes, we have paper and pencil work that we are completing during the week, but there is so much more.

Some of my most cherished memories are the years when I was homeschooled in the mountains of Virginia where I grew up. I had so much time with my sisters and was given the chance to explore, play, and be outside for hours at a time. My mom reading to us in the afternoons, our weekly visits to the library, and the opportunity to have an unhurried and analog childhood are precious memories that I hope to recreate in part for my own family.

If you're doubtful about starting or continuing the journey, I want to encourage you to know that you *are* equipped and have what it takes to homeschool your child if that is what the Lord is calling you to do. You are your child's first teacher. No matter where you are at in your homeschooling adventure, I want you to know that you are capable of doing this- and doing it well. Don't get caught up in what everyone else is doing. It's way too easy to hop on social media and see all the things we *think* we're doing wrong. It's easy to compare ourselves to other moms and what their days look like. It's a downward spiral that I'd encourage you not to pursue. It's helpful to seek inspiration and ideas from other people, but when it paralyzes us, causes us to feel like a failure, or we think we aren't doing enough, it no longer serves us.

In the age of social media, we can get lost in the highlight reels of other families. We see perfectly organized homeschool rooms, kids engaged in elaborate science experiments, and moms who seem to have it all together. It's natural to compare ourselves and wonder if we're falling short (ask me how I know). But remember, social media often shows only the best moments, not the struggles, the chaos, or the imperfect days.

When we constantly compare ourselves to others, we undermine our own unique journey. Each family is different and each child is different. What works for one may not work for another. Embrace your path and recognize the value in your individual experiences. Celebrate the small victories and progress that you and your children make each day.

Instead of focusing on what you think you're lacking, turn your attention to what you're achieving. Reflect on the reasons why you chose to homeschool and the goals you have for your family. Remember the joy and the learning that happens in the everyday moments, the bonds you're strengthening, and the unique opportunities you're providing for your children.

Setting boundaries with social media is crucial if it leaves you feeling inadequate or if you find yourself spending way too much time on a certain platform. I've learned this first-hand. Consider limiting your time on social media apps or taking breaks when you need to. Taking a break from apps by deleting them from your phone for a week or more can be incredibly refreshing. One book I really enjoy is *The 40-Day Social Media Fast* by Wendy Speake,[18] and I turn to it whenever I take breaks from social media. I do this at least once or twice a year. Nothing compares to face-to-face connection with other mom friends *in real life* who can offer genuine support and encouragement.

Regarding comparison, I've noticed that judgment and stereotypes can arise from both sides. Parents with children in public schools might sense that homeschooling families view public education as inferior or inadequate. On the other hand, families who homeschool may feel judged by those in the public school system for their decision to educate their children at home or for perceived socialization issues.

I have very close friendships with moms who send their kids to both public and private schools. One of my sisters, an educator at a local public Collegiate School, was recently awarded Teacher of the Year. I am incredibly proud of her and the admirable work she does for her students. My decision to homeschool doesn't imply any judgment toward my friends who don't. What if we all decided to support and encourage each other as moms, regardless of how we choose to educate our children? Imagine the strength we could find

---

[18] Speake, Wendy. *The 40-Day Social Media Fast: Exchange Your Online Distractions for Real-Life Devotion.* Baker Books, 2020.

in unity, understanding that each family makes the best decision for their unique circumstances. Instead of allowing differences to divide us, let's focus on our shared goals: raising happy, healthy, respectful, God-honoring children.

In my homeschooling journey, I've learned the value of mutual respect and the importance of celebrating each other's choices. Supporting each other as moms means offering a listening ear and showing empathy. It's about recognizing that every educational path has its own set of challenges and rewards. By building each other up, we can create a community where every mom feels valued and supported, no matter how they choose to educate their children.

Let's aim to be beacons of hope for one another, offering encouragement and understanding. Together, we can foster an environment where all educational choices are respected and every mom feels confident and capable in her unique journey.

It's natural to question if you're doing enough or if you are equipped for this home education journey. But remember, your love, dedication, and willingness to learn alongside your child are more than enough. Every challenge you face, and every solution you find helps create a meaningful educational experience. You don't have to have all the answers or be a perfect teacher. Your commitment to your child's growth and reaching their heart is what truly matters. Be confident in your abilities and celebrate your progress each week.

There's a comforting invitation for us from Jesus in Matthew 11:28-30 (NIV), "Come to me, all you who are weary and burdened, and I will give you rest. Take my yoke upon you and learn from me, for I am gentle and humble in heart, and you will find rest for your souls. For my yoke is easy and my burden is light."

I'm not sure about you, but I often need *soul rest*. These words serve as a reminder to lean on Jesus for strength and renewal. As we trust in Him and seek His guidance in our educational decisions, we can find rest for our weary hearts and assurance that His grace sustains us through every challenge. These words remind us that when we feel worn out, Jesus is there to lighten the load. So, as we navigate another school year, leaning on Him brings us peace and the strength to keep going.

During your homeschooling journey, it's important to spend some time each year planning- starting with the end in mind as you approach each school year. I'm a firm believer in having a vision for *why* you are homeschooling because that vision and your why will help carry you on your hardest homeschooling days. Especially on the days you want to quit and you begin to question your sanity! While having a clear vision and establishing a purpose for your homeschooling year is crucial, it's equally important to remain flexible and adaptable throughout the year.

One of the greatest blessings of homeschooling is the flexibility it offers. We can tailor the curriculum to fit our children's individual learning styles, interests, and paces. We recognize that every child is unique and that what works for one may not work for another. It's okay to deviate from the traditional methods and create a learning environment that fosters curiosity, wonder, and joy. Each child learns at their own pace. Flexibility allows you to slow down or accelerate based on your child's comprehension and mastery of subjects.

Life is unpredictable, with unexpected events like illnesses, family emergencies, or other disruptions. For example, we had planned a family day at a local botanical garden where we were going to incorporate science, math, and reading into our school day. One of the girls woke up with a stomach bug, and as bummed as I was that our day didn't go as planned, I knew we could pivot and try again a few days later. Flexibility and a backup plan will help you adjust your schedule and maintain continuity in your child's education. When other learning opportunities, like field trips, community events, or teachable moments come up, being flexible allows you to make the most of these experiences for enhanced learning.

Another thing to consider is that your children's interests and passions can, and probably will, change over time. Adapting your curriculum to incorporate their current interests keeps them engaged and motivated to learn. There's one specific example of this that makes me laugh every time I think about it.

Last year, one of my friends introduced "Leif the Lucky" to her kids as part of their U.S. History studies. They delved into the fascinating world of Leif Erikson and the Vikings, which sparked an unexpected wave of enthusiasm among her kids. They eagerly devoured every Viking book from the library shelves. Inspired by their interest, my friend transformed their planned one-week study into a rich, *six-week* thematic unit centered around Viking culture. Six weeks!

What was initially planned as a one-week study soon blossomed into a six-week exploration.

During this extended period, they not only explored Viking history but also ventured into learning about Norway and the Northern Lights. Embracing the flexibility of interest-led learning, my friend adapted her curriculum to accommodate their deepening curiosity. She shared that letting go of some control and allowing the curriculum to evolve organically was challenging yet immensely rewarding. For my sweet friend, this experience highlighted the power of interest-led learning in fostering genuine enthusiasm and meaningful exploration. The flexibility of interest-led learning allowed her children to delve deeply into a topic they were passionate about, fostering a rich educational experience that went far beyond textbooks and worksheets.

I want my girls to be lifelong learners. And one of the primary goals of homeschooling is to nurture a lifelong love of learning. This involves creating a stimulating and engaging environment where education is seen as a natural and enjoyable part of life. By making learning fun and relevant, we can help our children develop a deep-seated curiosity and enthusiasm for discovering new things. I often tell my girls that "the world is our classroom," and learning can happen outside our four walls.

Integrate learning into daily life by using everyday activities as teaching moments and encourage your children to explore topics they are passionate about. Take advantage of natural learning opportunities such as gardening, cooking, and nature walks to teach science, math, and other subjects. Encourage them to pursue their interests and provide them with resources and opportunities to explore new topics. By fostering a love for learning, you can help your children develop the skills and mindset needed to become lifelong learners.

Last year, writer and podcaster Abbie Halberstadt released a book titled *Hard Is Not the Same Thing as Bad: The Perspective Shift That Could Completely Change the Way You Mother*.[19] I read it a few months ago after completing a somewhat challenging homeschooling year. While reading Abbie's book, I realized that my mindset, attitude, and perspective were largely responsible for some of the challenges we faced.

Homeschooling isn't always easy—far from it. Some days are incredibly tough. But those challenging days don't define the experience as negative. Even on the hardest homeschooling days, amidst the struggle, I've learned to seek out the good and practice gratitude for the small, precious moments that make it all worthwhile.

If you feel like you might not be doing enough or are questioning whether you're ready for this journey, this is totally normal. But here's the thing — your love, dedication, and willingness to learn alongside your child? They're more than enough. Every challenge you face and every solution you figure out? They all add up to creating a meaningful and impactful educational experience. You don't have to have all the answers or be a perfect teacher. What matters is your willingness, commitment, and efforts.

---

[19] Halberstadt, Abbie. *Hard Is Not the Same Thing as Bad: The Perspective Shift That Could Completely Change the Way You Mother*. Bethany House Publishers, 2023.

Here are just a few things to consider, no matter where you are in your homeschooling journey.

1. Pray through the decision to homeschool each year.

Prayer allows us to seek God's wisdom and discernment in making such a significant decision. It opens our hearts to listen to God's leading and align our plans with His will. Prayer helps us clarify our priorities and values, ensuring we make decisions that align with our family's beliefs and goals.

Homeschooling is a commitment that can vary in duration based on family circumstances and children's needs. Through prayer, we can discern the ideal time to begin or continue homeschooling, ensuring our decisions are well-suited to our family's current needs and circumstances.

2. Seek guidance from a trusted mentor or friend.

Before we decided to start homeschooling, I went to lunch with one of my mentors. I wanted to ask her about her experiences, as I knew she had insight and wisdom to share. I also knew her kids weren't always homeschooled and did both private and public school throughout their school years. If you know someone who has been homeschooling for a while, see if you can take them out for coffee or lunch. Or, invite them over to your house. Ask them about their curriculum choices, planning tips, and homeschooling methodologies. If you're a seasoned homeschool mom, having a trusted mentor or friend can help offer a fresh perspective on various situations, offer new ideas, or give suggestions that you might not have considered.

3. *Locate and build community.*

This might be the most important part of homeschooling, and I cannot stress enough the importance of having community. Whether you're part of a co-op, a homeschool community, a hybrid school, or a gathering with a couple of friends, it will help provide a network of support. This is where you can connect with like-minded families and find encouragement, friendships, and shared experiences, which is an invaluable part of this experience. We have a built-in community through our hybrid school, and I am so grateful for it.

If you don't know where to start, use a search engine to look up "homeschool co-ops or communities near me." or search Facebook Groups and see where you can get plugged in. Or maybe you start your own group! I live 30-40 minutes from almost everything, but it's always worth the drive to do life with friends. Isolation can be a breeding ground for resentment and depression. Home education is so much more fulfilling and uplifting when done with friends and in a community.

4. *Attend a conference or an event.*

Most states have some kind of annual conference for home-educating families. You can also check the websites of major homeschool organizations, such as the Home School Legal Defense Association (HSLDA)[20], which often lists upcoming events. With the rise of online events, many organizations now offer virtual homeschool conferences, which can be attended from anywhere, regardless of your state. As

---

[20] https://hslda.org/

moms, we pour out so much on a daily basis, and conferences can be such a refreshing time filled with encouragement and inspiration. If you're able to coordinate going with a group of other moms, it makes for a fun getaway, too! A happy and healthy mom is a vital part of a successful homeschooling experience.

5. Know that you won't know everything- and that's okay!

As a homeschooling mom, you're on an adventure that is uniquely yours. There is no one-size-fits-all approach to homeschooling. What works for one family might not work for another, and that's perfectly okay. Remember, *no one knows your child better than you do*. Try to embrace the flexibility that homeschooling offers and celebrate the small victories along the way. There will be days filled with questions, uncertainties, and unexpected challenges. But in these moments of doubt, growth happens — both for you and your child. Don't be afraid to admit when you don't know something; view it as an opportunity to learn together. This not only models a lifelong love of learning but shows your child that asking for help is normal.

Friend, continue doing the good work He has called you to, and remember that the harvest will come. When doubts and fears arise, surrender them to God and rest in His peace. He knows your heart, your struggles, and your desires. He is faithful, and He will carry you through. Embrace the journey with faith, knowing you are walking in God's purpose. Your dedication, love, and faith are sowing seeds that will bear fruit for eternity. Keep your eyes on Him, and remember that your work is not in vain. Above all, remember that God has a unique and perfect plan for your family. If He has called you to this journey, He will equip you with everything you need.

And, if no one else has told you this lately, let me be the one to tell you: You are doing a great job, momma. I'm in your corner, and I'm cheering you on.

About the

Authors

*

About the

Authors

*

Jamie Inman

A veteran homeschool mom, Jamie lives in the delightful hills of southern West Virginia with her husband and seven children. When not schooling her brood, she can be found tending her other "kids", a herd of wily but charming goats, or running trails in the enchanting forests close to her home. Writing is a new passion that has grown from an old dream that began in childhood when she had a poem published in the local newspaper. Leaning on almost two decades of teaching and homeschooling experience, she desires to share the knowledge she has gleaned with other moms in the trenches of the school years.

Connect with Jamie

Facebook & Instagram: @Jamie.Inman.Writer

Website: www.Jamie-Inman.com

Keri Lynn Willis M.Ed.

Keri is married to her magnificent husband of almost 40 years, Harold. They live in San Diego with their lively Weimaraner, Belle, and serve in leadership at their church home. They have two happily married children and one granddaughter. Keri is a graduate of Liberty University and has a Master's in Education from San Diego State University. She has worked in various areas of education and ministry, with a special place in her heart for individuals with special needs. She enjoys teaching God's children of all ages and loves all things outdoors. Her favorite "office" is her backyard, where many ideas for women's retreats, speaking engagements, blog posts, and books have been born. You can find Keri's books on Amazon.

Connect with Keri

Instagram: @kerilynnwillis

Facebook: Keri Willis

Pinterest: @keriwillis

Website: kerilynnwillis.com

Anna Dabill

Anna Dabill, RDN, started blogging, took a 4-month traveling sabbatical, and moved to VA from MN in the empty nest transition. She works part-time and is working on future picture books. Anna and her husband graduated from NDSU, have three adult kids, and love hiking, cooking, gardening, stand-up paddle boarding, and nature. Anna's blog focuses on Faith, Food, Family, Fun, and Favorites.

Connect with Anna

Blog: Dabillaroundthetable.com

Facebook: @dabillaroundthetable

Instagram: @dabillanna

Kayren J. Cathcart

Kayren J. Cathcart is a wife, mother, and psalmist who is learning the joy of obeying God's will in every facet and season of her life. As a creative soul who's worked in a corporate environment for more than two decades, Kayren has become a relentless advocate for self-care and total wellness. A self-professed recovering people-pleaser and overachiever, Kayren is dedicated to helping women enhance their personal effectiveness through spiritual growth and leadership development. She's fluent in emoji and believes that glitter should be an integral part of every day. With wit and wisdom, Kayren enjoys sharing her observations on daily life and "the ministry of the mundane."

Connect with Kayren

Blog: https://kayrencathcart.com/

LinkedIn and Pinterest: Kayren Cathcart

YouTube: @kayrencathcart

Podcast: Paper Polisher

Énid Meyer Tchir

É nid Meyer Tchir (pronounced Ā-nid) is passionate about inspiring women of all ages in their faith and encouraging them to believe that God can do anything, even in tough times. With a degree in English and a minor in Film, she has counseled hundreds of women while serving in full-time ministry for over two decades. A dynamic public speaker, Ènid is also the creator and co-host of the podcast The Well. She lives in Atlanta with her handsome husband and amazing college-aged son.

Connect with Ènid

Instagram: @etchir

Nikki Tigg

Nikki Tigg is a wife, mom, writer, speaker, and encourager.

She is passionate about helping women grow in their love for God by helping them learn more about God. Nikki enjoys speaking to teens and women of all ages and stages. She does this through leading small group, writing devotionals, speaking on podcasts, and at conferences.

Nikki is relaunching her podcast, Constant Surrender, which encourages women to surrender to Jesus' leading one decision at a time.

Connect with Nikki

Instagram: @nikkitigg and @constant_surrender

Website: www.nikkitigg.com

Bonnie Shue McDonald

Bonnie McDonald has a passion for prayer and discipleship. During 15 years of youth ministry at Mt. Pleasant Methodist Church, she helped many parents and students navigate the transitional years to middle and high school. Currently, she serves there as a church leader in discipleship and shares her prayer-filled stories. She encourages others to share theirs. She lives in North Carolina with her husband, Flint, and they have two adult children and one grandchild.

Connect with Bonnie

Instagram: @faithfulinnc

Facebook: Bonnie Shue McDonald

Website: www.bonniesmcdonald.com

Takhia Gaither

*T*akhia Gaither is a 20+ year STEM educator who used skills learned while being a classroom teacher to create a profitable and growing book editing, formatting, and writing/book coaching business, The Ready Write-Her Writing Services. A multi-time Amazon best-selling author and editor, she is also a mom of 2, in ministry at her church, and is pursuing her Doctor of Education in Educational Psychology. Takhia holds an AA in Teacher Education, a BS in Mathematics, an MS in Information Technology, and coaching certifications in life coaching, confidence coaching, and mental health coaching.

Connect with Takhia

Facebook/Instagram: @takhiatheteacher

X Twitter: @ttheteach

TikTok: @thereadywriteher

Website: thereadywriteher.com

Amy E. Dyster

*B*orn and raised in Jacksonville, Florida, Amy has a deep love and appreciation for people and their stories. She graduated from Florida State University with a degree in Marketing and from the University of Georgia with a Masters in English Education. Amy served on the staff of Campus Crusade for Christ (now known as Cru) for five years, working in Italy with students at the University of Pisa and stateside at both of her alma maters. Amy teaches high school English and lives in the Atlanta area with her two children and yellow lab. She enjoys spending time with her family, traveling, reading, and relaxing on the beach.

Connect with Amy

Instagram: @amydphillips78

Chelsea Garofalo

Chelsea lives in southwest Florida with her husband of 15 years, and their two spirited daughters. They're a Jesus-loving, first generation ranch family that enjoys outdoor adventures and the flexibility that homeschooling provides.

When she's not chasing chickens or cows, Chelsea loves working out at the YMCA, reading, and going to their local beaches. She is passionate about clean living and wellness, and she supports and encourages moms through authentic conversation and connection (preferably over an oat milk cappuccino).

Chelsea is the creator of Gather + Grow, a community offering a variety of gatherings designed to encourage, inspire, and support moms as they grow in their walk with the Lord and as home educators.

Connect with Chelsea

Instagram: @theranchmom

Looking to *connect* with a
community of writers?

hope✳writers
www.hopewriters.com

The world needs your *hope-filled* words
more now than ever before.

Thinking about *writing*
your own book?

hope✳books
www.hopebooks.com

Made in the USA
Middletown, DE
24 August 2024